A New Paradigm for Humanity

Dennis Lusk

To all my fellow humans:
May we survive not only as a species but as the only creators of
technology that can build new worlds.

Table of contents

Preface

AS I LOOK at the world around me, news and current events, I am troubled by the future that we humans are creating. There are criminal governments stealing as much as they can from their citizenry, producing debt that will continue forever. Big government is being seen as a solution to all problems when, in reality, many of those problems are created by the governments themselves. They are colluding with international corporations for the sole benefit of the owners of the corporations. Governments and corporations are becoming ever larger and more powerful and none dare call it fascism.

Countries once wealthy with skilled populations have become welfare states with more people getting a check from the government than there are productive workers. Governments are supporting large non-working classes and are even more the default employer. The problem becomes that there are fewer productive citizens to create real wealth. To allow this to continue, there are only two possibilities, one is ever more taxes on an already overburdened citizenry. The other is ever more debt that must increase exponentially eroding investments, savings and retirement.

There are economic and hot wars for control of resources by large countries against smaller less wealthy countries. The people in few areas are allowed to determine their future and the future of their children. Propaganda generated by governments cultivates the belief in a beneficent government. The same source of propaganda begets such things as extreme socialism, racism, and extreme environmentalism. These make an excuse for government to grow ever larger and powerful. Political dogmas are becoming pseudo religions while some actual historically rooted religions are becoming radicalized. Lacking any other political outlet in many parts of the world, religion is being used to unify and motivate.

There was recently a picture taken by the spacecraft Messenger, looking back toward the Earth from Mercury. It looked very tiny and alone and it was humbling to think that everyone alive today, in fact, everyone who has ever lived was on that little dot. The only reassurance was that our Moon was in the same picture and that, someday, people will live there too. The goal for humanity is, for me, very clear. We must move, at least, some people off the Earth. It must be THE primary goal of humanity.

This is the age of the Internet, the ubiquitous network, which is available to most people on the planet. I have done most of my research on-line and have verified it from many sources. Indeed, there is a great deal of misinformation and propaganda out there but that is also true of books. Since this book is conjecture about a different path to the future, not every point was referenced. If there are statements that are found to be confusing or thought to be in error, you are invited to look it up as I have. Be sure to check domestic and foreign sources and weigh the veracity of the information. In fact, I certainly hope that you are concerned enough to care. Go to any library or Internet search engine and have a look, it only takes a few seconds, and you will be as rewarded. One does need to be careful of controversial subjects as there are many opinions and you are free to choose your own; but choose wisely.

The purpose of this book is to show that we cannot continue to scrap and scrape for survival on a single planet. We need to start building an interplanetary civilization and it can begin now. We have the technology; all we need is the will.

The chapters in this book are generally laid out with a chapter explaining the problem or problems and the next chapter is what is available as a better way, then how can we do better in the future. The better ways are the new paradigm. The biggest question is, what do we want the future to be for the children of today and of humans yet unborn?

Paradigm

"You can ignore reality but you cannot ignore the consequences of ignoring reality."

~ AYN RAND

THERE IS LITTLE doubt that a single factory, perhaps in China, could manufacture every cooking pot needed in the world. As the cost of automation continues to come down there will be fewer jobs for even low cost human workers. Even in China, robots are doing much of the factory work. There are less and less people needed on the assembly lines of the world. The same applies to just about every other manufactured product. There are ever fewer manufacturing jobs and the majority of those jobs are highly technical requiring education, training and most importantly self-motivation.

In primitive hunter-gather societies, every member of the tribe was important because of the labor required to collect needed calories. An empty belly is a great motivator and will inspire even the most indolent individual into action. The invention of agriculture cheapened the cost of labor because less people were needed to keep the community fed. When the fields didn't need tending, serfs could be used for construction projects such as pyramids, temples, palaces, aqueducts, roads and great walls. They could also be used for wars to attack neighbors.

Agricultural methodologies progressed thru the years and fewer people were needed to tend to the fields, altho it was still a large percentage of the population. There were extra people so professional armies could be supported by their labors to defend and expand kingdoms, create empires and keep the elites in power. Human muscles were used for most efforts. There were some animals used but they were much more expensive and more difficult to control than humans were. Humans were so cheap and prolific that there were mass starvations because the elites and their armies controlled the food supplies and their needs came first. If there were too many serfs, they would be killed or allowed to starve to death; this has continued into modern times.

There were events in the late Middle Ages that changed the human labor paradigm and that was the great plagues. There have been many plagues and mass deaths. As late as 1920 the Spanish Flu epidemic killed almost five percent of the world's population, most in the industrialized countries. The Black Death was the most severe and exterminated huge populations killing twenty percent of the world's population and as many as seventy percent of Europeans. Human labor became so expensive that it started the "Renaissance", or rebirth, and set the stage for the industrial revolution. Let us hope for a brighter future where, at least, this chapter of history does not need to repeat itself.

Because of the plagues, humans became valuable and it became cheaper to use machinery. The modern era began because trained technicians were needed to build and maintain the machines. The literacy rate in Western Europe rose quickly thru the Eighteenth and Nineteenth Centuries as the industrial revolution was spreading. It was the industrialization of Europe that set them on the path to world domination. This situation is now being reversed because of the availability of cheap labor, mass production and robotics worldwide.

In the wealthier parts of the world as few as one percent of the population do the work of farming. The processes are highly mechanized. The trend to ever more machinery is spreading around the world especially in the planting and harvesting of grasses, including wheat, corn and rice, which provide most of the food for humans and our farm animals. The cost of food would rise considerably if human labor were still used to produce the quantities needed. It would rise so high that many parts of the world would again be facing starvation.

Mechanized farming has not progressed to the point where all fruits and vegetables are picked, sorted and packed by machine. Poorly educated migrants are imported from other areas. Admittedly, it does take a paycheck from locals who would benefit from having work. It is still pseudo slave labor because they are disposable; that is, easily replaced by another. There is the advantage of having cheaper foods if the locals can still afford them because they don't have any work. There would not be that much of an increase in cost if locals were used and laborers were paid better.

A migrant farm worker will receive, at most, about two percent of the cost of, for example, a tomato. In the United States they receive an average of about twenty dollars a kilogram. It is good wages considering the skill level, but is seasonal, usually eight months per year. Migrant farm workers receive approximately $7500 per year. If the wages were tripled to $22,500, the cost of the tomato would increase by less than four percent. One wonders why local labor could not be used, pay them better and keep the wealth in the community.

Manufactured products are similar, in the past low cost workers have been imported. Now, there is a migration of industrial jobs from high cost unionized and high tax areas to less expensive labor and low tax areas. The reason why this is happening is very simple; the same product can be made for lower cost. It will also increase the profitability and competitiveness of the company. Then again, if low cost workers can't be bred, as they have been in the past, imported from another area or otherwise procured then why not manufacture them too?

Robots are being used for many jobs from building automobiles to answering phone calls. Who hasn't been subjected to the questioning of a computerized answering machine that every large company seems to have? They have progressed from a simple statement followed by a request to press a number to be routed to your area of concern, to understanding spoken words. Of course, one has to speak clearly and enunciate with one word answers being preferred. There are long lists of possibilities, starting with "If you want pay your bill press 1" to being deep into a phone tree and have the call dropped. Are people really so expensive that they can't be trained to direct a phone call?

Robots with "intelligence" are being developed that would replace humans in even more situations. It is difficult to see the point of developing artificial intelligence... if it is even possible. Why take jobs and a paycheck from some humans to enrich others? One can see some need for computers and some robotic manufacturing if the job is repetitive and requires precision but not intelligence. Machines could only imperfectly simulate human brains and could not have the same sort of intellect. Humans are capable of soaring imagination, creativity and amazing problem solving abilities. Good workers, even those on assembly lines, can correct problems as they come to them. One should be against anything that demeans human life. People are everything; what is the point of building a brighter future for robots?

On the other hand, some people have been taught that governments will always provide for them. They are "entitled" to live with the appearance of being middle class when, in fact, they are living on handouts. In the United States alone, more than half of all households have a member receiving government "benefits". These benefits give the recipients a place to live, a full belly and great deal of idle time. Many of these recipients live in poorly maintained and policed government housing. They are forced to live with other people who live on handouts and it becomes a culture on its own. A culture where one is considered an outcast if school and career is a goal.

In many cases, the only way for a woman to get a larger "paycheck" is to have more children. The path to success for men is to join a gang and become thieves, drug dealers or killers. This situation has become so bad in the United States that it has more people, per capita, incarcerated than anywhere else in the world. Where are all of those criminals coming from? They are the products of the so-called social welfare system. These people could be doing things important to themselves and all humanity instead of being given tools to be destructive by their own government. Worse, it is being paid for by current and future taxpayers.

One of the biggest problems in the so-called industrialized world is that the least motivated, uneducated and government dependent continue to outbreed the productive. In the modern world many are kept by the government in good health but are not required to anything except be faithful to the government. The Russians have a phrase for it, "novy sovetsky chelovek" – new soviet man. The slang for this phrase is "sovki" or scoop (hollow out?), but it is part of life in most every "modern" country. If this continues for generations, it will certainly affect their adaptability.

There was a science fiction movie made in 2006, "Idiocracy", a story about two underachievers from the present time who were put into hibernation. They were awakened five hundred years in the future to find a world peopled by the dim-witted. There were problems everywhere, but no one had the intelligence to solve them. Because of government actions, poor education, incessant commercialism and a culture of idiocy, it was a future where the stupid had become the norm. It was a homogeneous society without any intellectual curiosity and any independent thought. After watching what seems to be an entertaining comedy, but is actually tragic if this is to be our future. Then you come to realize the real tragedy is that this is a commentary on our world as it is now. The screenplay was written with Americans in mind; who are, in general, are the most entertained but the poorest informed people in the world.

Unconditional government handouts are not the best way to aid people who need help. Human beings are the most adaptable creatures on earth, give them a chance; dependence as with all creatures, except parasites, will destroy them. The government subsidized irresponsibility and indolence must stop or we will destroy ourselves.

Swedish professor Hans Rosling, in a TED lecture, made some very good points about economic development. He said that the population of the world could be economically divided into four groups. The first and poorest group of about two billion people heats water with fire. The second group of three billion people lives by light from electricity. A third group of about a billion can purchase airline tickets and have a plethora of machinery in their homes; they are the richest. There is a fourth group in between the electricity group and the airline group. They are wealthier than the group that has electric light but they can't afford an airline ticket. They are about one billion people that have the economic wherewithal to purchase a washing machine.

Dr. Rosling mentioned that these groups are divided by energy usage. He also mentioned that it would be difficult to convince the people with electric light that they can't have a washing machine because of environmental concerns. What must happen in the future is the average wealth of individuals increase. The washing machine group wants to be able to purchase airline tickets and fill their homes with electric appliances. They will do what they need to do to become part of that group and the richest group will double to two billion. They will also massively increase world energy usage because even now this group uses seven times the energy of the rest.

The three billion people with electricity will want their washing machine and they, the largest group, will double their energy use. The population of the Earth is still increasing with the majority of the increase at the poorest group. In the next few years, the fire group will grow from two billion to about four billion. They may have access to a radio or even a television in their village or nearby and they have electric light. They will even hope to, someday, get a washing machine.

There is an enormous pressure to increase the energy supplies of the world and make it available to all people of the world. The result of this increase in the use of energy is not just more danger to the environment, which can be resolved, but an uplifting of people. When people don't have backbreaking work all day they will want to learn things and improve their lives even further. Education becomes the most important thing in their lives. Humans need goals and intellectual challenges to thrive.

There is much work to be done because in the airline group there is some real craziness promoted by the media and even government programs. Again, they actively promote criminality and drug addiction. Being poor is not synonymous with criminality; there was far less crime during the so-called Great Depression than there is now. The role of the popular media in promoting drugs and gangsterism is nothing less than shocking. As a watcher of culture, I saw the expansion of drug use throughout the 1970's and 80's. It remains part of the culture promoted by the popular media. Today, marijuana smokers are almost as common as cigarette smokers. There is a movement underway to legalize drug usage in the capital of the United States. The pernicious influence of the "popular" media goes even beyond drug abuse but also disseminates misinformation about news and politics and inspires hysteria about such things as diverse as socialism, global "warming" and genetically modified organisms.

Actions by some corporations in cooperation with the media are also destructive. For example, bottled water costs ten thousand times as much as tap water, has more bacteria and it produces over twenty million tons of plastic waste worldwide. We are told that we should drink eight glasses (bottles) of water per day which is too much without exercising. In addition, bottled water is actually derived from...

"filtered" tap water. The plastic bottles end up as trash in the streets, streams, rivers and eventually the oceans where it is concentrated by ocean currents. There are islands of floating plastic; the largest one is in the North Pacific that is twice as large as France or Texas.

Most of humanity, because of actions of the elites and their minions in the government and the media are unable to see the need to get off our home planet when there is infinitely more out there. The vast majority of humanity is unable to improve their condition. Ordinary people see themselves as powerless while the elites are only interested in advancing their own positions. The elites that control governments, with their moral relativism, are in a constant struggle to maintain their wealth and control.

Many believe that the efforts of the so-called progressives and social engineers who have been trying to create "socialist" man from their mold have been a failure for humanity. They have, in many ways, succeeded with the millions who live on government social programs who know no other way to live. These people do not progress humanity toward a brighter future. They, in fact, retard it because of the astronomical amounts of money needed for their support with no return on the investment.

Where are the jobs of the future for the mass of humanity? We can only hope they are not fighting endless wars for less and less resources. Humanity must have some sort of goal something that gives them dignity and makes the future worthwhile. There must be a different path for humankind, a new paradigm.

The human brain, for all its foibles, and however it works, it does work extremely well. We think, feel, dream, invent and can see things happening before they happen. We have created agriculture, temples and space stations. We do far more than just muddle through. As Carl Sagan said, "We are the Universe contemplating itself". Perhaps, there are those who wish us to remain on this planet and end progress for most of humankind. That is not only irrational, but also pure evil.

All of humanity is in one place, one planet. It is the ultimate irresponsibility to not consider future generations of humanity and act while capable of acting. We have a small window of time in which to move; we cannot take a chance on losing our ability to do so. It is counter to this goal that people be addicted to government handouts, idleness and drugs. There is a better path, better ways and they are available to us now. Many of these ways will be discussed but they are not the only the approach to getting where we want to be.

Human greed can be harnessed to achieve positive results. An enterprise with the goal of moving people to the Moon and out into the Solar System will be the greatest endeavor conceived. There is much work for everyone that is interested from the most humble worker to administrators, engineers and scientists. Work enough for generations and generations and once put into motion will continue. It may be possible to show the elites that if anything happens to the Earth or civilization they are just as doomed as the rest of us. There is no place to hide.

We have now reached a point that has never been reached before; we can evolve ourselves. The Earth egg needs to hatch. We need to stop our petty wars for control of each other's resources to enrich a few. It is time to uplift all of humanity and spread our seed of intelligence beyond the planet Earth. We evolved with the creatures of the Earth and we can assure their future too.

Dystopia

You can rule ignorance; you can manipulate the illiterate; you can do whatever you want when a people are uneducated, so that goes in line with corrupt business and corrupt politics.

~W<small>ILL</small>.<small>I</small>.<small>AM</small>

IF HUMANITY IS to move forward with a new paradigm there are situations that need to be corrected or, at least, ameliorated. One of the situations is that there is apathy, even hostility, toward culture and education in many areas including the United States that is promoted by the media. Educational systems are dominated by politics and the agendas set by the politicians. Humanity needs to move forward to a better future but many politicians want to breed people as "voters" to keep them in power. Students are indoctrinated by government control of schools as well as the unionized teachers who follow the party line.

In the United States, schools were previously controlled by local communities but in the name of "improving" and "standardizing" education they have come under the purview of an overarching federal government dominated by politicians. Their largest concerns are not education but maintaining their personal power and, yes, money. The schools are an ideal place to begin indoctrination of future citizens in a particular political ideology. The agendas involve teaching of the blind acceptance of such things as history rewritten by the people in power and that big government is the best government. Schools are even used to promote one political party over another.

In the United States, educational excellence has been falling compared to other industrialized nations since the Department of Education was created in 1979 by President Jimmy Carter. It now has an enormous budget of seventy billion dollars and a staff of over five thousand. This budget is in addition to State and local educational spending which averages over twelve thousand dollars per student. Educational costs in the United States are tied with the most expensive country Switzerland, which is always close to number one in education excellence. What do students in the United States gain for all this money spent? In a list of nations, high school seniors in the United States ranked twenty-sixth in mathematics, twenty-fourth in general science and close to last in physics. Worse, only five percent of seventeen-year-old students could read and use information found in technical, historical and other documents.

There has been a huge decline in the number of students that score well on verbal scholastical aptitude tests. Only six percent of high school juniors could solve basic algebra problems. Less than half knew when Lincoln was President, and far fewer that he was a Republican. High school education is so poor that all institutions of higher learning provide remedial education to prepare them for college courses. Charlotte Thomson Iserbyt, former Senior Policy Advisor in the United States Department of Education, blew the whistle on government activities that are deliberately lowering educational standards across the United States. It is truly criminal but it is unlikely that the bureaucrats and politicians will ever be brought to justice.

Many published statistics say schools in the United States are in good shape and student goals are within established parameters. One can look at various documents that rate educational excellence, for example, according to the CIA Factbook (2001), the United States has 99% literacy rate. However, a report by the National Assessment of Adult Literacy (2002) states that "...the resultant literacy rate for the United States would be, at most 65-85%...". A report by USA Today in 2009 stated that more than 1 in 7 Americans do not have the ability to read their paper. This is the problem; the academics that establish the parameters and goals are the same as those that do the measuring. They have caused the reduction in educational excellence to further their big government agendas and the money that it brings.

Universities and colleges are generally socialistic in their outlook and it is promoted and passed along to students. This penchant for big government socialism goes back to the 1920's, where self-styled intellectual revolutionaries were working toward change. A change from the old world where the elites, royalty and industrialists, controlled the world. In their view, it would be changed to the new world where the "common man" would control the world guided by the self same intellectuals. This worldview created socialism, fascism, communism and the bloody Twentieth Century where hundreds of millions died. This same perverted worldview still exists but only as tools of the elites promoted by a mendacious money hungry academia.

The meddling of the United States Federal government has results that are inconsistent and discriminatory. The Federal controlled educational system remains extremely racist. The United States has some of the best universities in the world but some of the worst school systems. In America's largest cities, where most of African Americans live, high schools graduate less than half of the students. There is a reason for this; poor educational systems will create a dependent underclass that can be counted on to support the local gangsters, which is apparently the goal.

There is an intolerable situation in the Democratic Party's hegemony of Detroit and similar situations in other cities in the United States. Until the 1960's, Detroit was the industrial capital of the world and the fourth largest city in the US. The corruption has been so bad for so long more that half the population has left and half of those that remain can no longer read and less than twenty percent graduate from High School. It lacks adequate services including police and has one of the highest murder rates in the world. It makes no sense that the population, as a block, votes democratic. Most big cites in America are not far behind. How bad does it have to become before citizens want shady politics out of their cities and out of their schools? Poor education truly begets an anti-utopia.

Schools were forced by the government to have affirmative action programs to promote so-called racial equality. They were then required to pass a certain percentage of "minorities" whether or not they were qualified, which is the covert racism of lowered expectations. There have been some successes but overall what has been done is reduce educational excellence for all students. These programs appear push overall grades up, but it is another fabrication.

One must reject the government and media supported notion that so-called minorities are somehow inferior. They are required to live in an environment created for them by the government. The United States maintains government supported racism to this day thru a myriad of governmental programs. The worst result of this racism being dependence on the governmental and its role in education. It is evident in the declining ratings of educational excellence that the actions of politicians have "dumbed down" the schools to the least common denominator. It gives the illusion of an education and provides a graduation certificate but is only useful for menial jobs.

Wealthy nations instead of giving "aid" to poor nations in the form of billions of dollars in weapons systems should help provide education and especially female education. Male education is needed to have the skills to move their family toward a better position in society but educating women is also the best method of reducing the birthrate and overpopulation. Women provide most of the learning opportunities for the next generation. Female education can also reduce the amount of venereal disease. In South Africa and many other countries including the United States female high school students have "Sugar Daddies". They are older men who take advantage of them. In South Africa as much as one forth of female high school students has been infected with HIV. It is far too common in many places around the world. Education can slow the traffic in human slavery, both labor and the sex trade.

The problem is not the students but the policies of the academics and government control. Again in the United States, while European and Asian Americans in most areas do as well as higher ranked countries, African American students from inner cities and Latin Americans do poorly, pulling down the overall results. These groups, in the United States, have a culture of dependency enforced by the government of the United States and particularly the Democratic political party. These "disadvantaged" people are the group targeted to be used to keep corrupt politicians in power. There is much political sermonizing, but there is little effort to bring these students up to the level of others.

In Los Angeles, because of politics, aptitude testing of students is not even allowed. The authorities do not want to expose their incompetence and corruption and in what poor condition the learning process truly is. African American and Spanish speaking students do much worse than those with European or Asian ancestry. Because of this idiocy, it is not knowable which students are gifted and which have special needs. Most of the inner cities in America are just as shocking, with poor graduation rates or worse; students are graduated without basic skills. It is unconscionable, and the responsible people should be punished but are kept in power by a corrupt system.

Politicians including school board members, as always, say that the solution is more money. A large percentage of that "more money" ends up in their pockets or the pockets of cronies. Because of this, the cost of education has had little bearing on the quality. Washington, DC and California have some of the most expensive government schools in the world and, at the same time, the worst educational experience. It is blamed on students, which highlights the politician's racism. In reality, it is a culture that is nourished by the government and media not to value education and it results in a lack of discipline and educational excellence.

Education has been taken over by national governments much to the detriment of the schools, which have become little more than babysitters for disengaged students. Large segments of the population are more concerned with the lives of "celebrities" than the actions of their government that affect their own lives. Teachers and school staff are used by the politicians to keep them in power. The politicians in turn grant favors for organized teacher unions. In many places, the politicians use the government to fund unions; the unions in turn "donate" to the politician's election campaign. Unions become an arm of the political machine.

Ultimately, it is the taxpayer that funds the politician's power grab and it is educational system that suffers because the political machine protects the status quo. In the 2008 and 2012 United States elections, many teachers were actively campaigning in their classrooms for the Democratic Party and candidate who they perceived, rightly or wrongly, as the best for their union. Unfortunately, there is usually little parent or community oversight in government schools because the parents were raised in the same culture of ignorance.

Many government schools in the United States are not cost effective when the generally poor quality of the results is considered. Education is another cash cow for corrupt politicians. They fight tooth and nail to prevent any sort of voucher program that would allow children to go to better schools. Bankrupt California and the Los Angeles school district have built three new schools with amortized cost of almost twenty four thousand dollars per student per year. That is only the cost of the building; the cost of operation is far more.

Many school districts hide much of the cost of incompetence and corruption. In a review of the expenses in the five largest metro areas plus the District of Columbia found that, on average, the actual per student costs are almost fifty percent higher than that stated. According to the Cato Institute a considerable twenty-seven cents of every dollar collected at the state and local level is consumed by the government K to12 educational system. That number does not include even more Federal money to favored school districts for "special" programs. Why is it so expensive even with government subsidies and where does all the money go? Overpaid but sloppy management as well as "creative" accounting hide the payoffs, fraud and outright theft.

In the United States Colleges and Universities that are gifted with government subsidies, paradoxically, become even more gratuitously costly. Students must borrow considerable amounts of money to attend. The government is there to lend it to them without qualification so that American students are deeply in debt when they have completed their education. In the United States, there is an observable one to one correspondence between increasing government subsidies, increasing tuition costs and increasing costs of student loans. There is no doubt of collusion between a progressively more controlling government, higher education bribed with government money and banks providing government guaranteed loans all paid for by ever fewer productive taxpayers. The average college tuition cost is about fourteen thousand dollars per year; in other countries, it is much less costly. An example is Canada, where it is less than half at six thousand per year. In Germany, France and Scandinavia it is about one thousand dollars per year cost to the students and families. The United States ranks with so-called poor countries where there is a huge difference between the education of the rich and the poor.

Unions and tenure have the same goal and that is to maintain the officially protected status of a teacher's employment. That is, to protect teachers from parents and administrators. They also provide teachers with a good income with benefits. In the past teachers could have been dismissed for getting married, pregnant or even women wearing pants. Unions and tenure allow the teacher to speak up if they perceive a problem. They can provide teachers with a stable environment and allow them a certain amount of autonomy and the ability to make decisions about unruly students. It is particularly true with disciplinary problems with disruptive and inattentive students. In theory, they protect a good teacher from unwarranted discipline and dismissal but they also shelter poor teachers. In addition, administrators and community representatives should have a say in the demeanor of teachers and how children are educated.

Currently, tenure and unions are more often used to protect ineffective teachers and be a force for political goals. In many cases, unproductive or even criminal teachers are granted tenure automatically or by incompetent administrators. The removal of an incompetent teacher can be a complicated, lengthy and expensive process. They are locked into their positions no matter their effectiveness and educational excellence falls as a result. In New York State government schools, it costs a minimum of a quarter of a million dollars to remove an ineffective teacher. Some have histories of child molestation and have been on paid administrative leave for years. Because of the difficulties in removing them, problematic tenured teachers are paid to sit in "rubber" rooms doing nothing at a cost to New York taxpayers of almost a hundred million dollars per year. Union leaders have little concern for taxpayers or the education of students. Their goals as with all unions are money and power related.

In some school districts there are problems attracting good teachers because of discipline problems and even violence. This is especially true in the government dependent inner cities where programs force the poor who are also the most poorly educated into crime infested "developments". There is little concern for the future of the individuals or incentives to improve themselves. These government created dependence areas also require a long commute for the employees of inner city schools.

In these troubled areas, good teachers are hard to attract because of debased school reputations so high salaries and benefits would be needed. The unions will prevent it in the name of the "fairness" to other union members in better areas. In unionized government schools, all teachers receive the same salary based not upon excellence but upon time and not in the school system, but in the union. Teachers are not all qualified to teach all subjects and there is a problem attracting good science teachers because of union regulated wages. All this creates a situation where there is a particular lack of incentives to teachers to motivate students into learning needed skills.

Education has many positive aspects not only for the individual but for humanity as a whole. It will increase the wealth of the individuals and the nation. It will allow people to become productive citizens that keep a technological society running. Education of the next generation should be the most important goal of any society. It will cause the general uplifting of humanity so that there can be much more comprehensive participation in future endeavors. It is also the prerequisite for an honest and ethical government.

Education

Education is the most powerful weapon that you can
use to change the world.

~NELSON MANDELA

THERE IS A huge amount of knowledge available at this point in
time but there are far more unknowns to explore. It is unfortunate
that only a tiny percentage of humanity can appreciate and use this
information. Economics reveals that human capital is more important than physical capital for long-term economic development.
This is quite evident by the comparative economic power of highly
motivated and educated nations, which are generally poor in natural
resources, such as Finland, Japan, South Korea, Taiwan, Singapore,
Germany and Netherlands. In order for a nation to improve its wealth
and prosperity, it must make education the national priority. Finland
pays their teachers the highest in the world and they are respected
professionals like doctors and attorneys. It consistently shows up as
one of the top in rankings of educational excellence. Then again, they
are required to have the equivalent of a master's degree before they
can begin teaching.

Some nations are working toward a better-educated population, not leaving large segments of the population behind. Every
country has an educated segment that pulls the rest of the country
along but there are positive programs to increase that percentage.
The countries that have the most technologically advanced populations are places like Canada, Scandinavia, Netherlands, South Korea,
Japan, Taiwan, Malaysia and Singapore. The United States, Russia,
India, Brazil and China must be included as technology leaders simply because of their size, but they have a large part of their populations left behind for various reasons. Nevertheless, universal access
to higher education for qualified individuals is becoming more and
more common around the world.

It has been shown that tenure and teacher unions can be a detriment to educational excellence. An interesting concept as an alternative to tenure and unions would be to have associations of teachers,
professors and educational administrators run like a law firm. The
firm would have a contract with a school, private or government, for
a number of people that would provide specific services. The firm
would take responsibility for its members as well as handle pay and
pensions. The school would negotiate with the firm and it would
negotiate with the members. One of the big advantages is that public and private schools would have access to the same pool of talent.
Good teachers would be protected by contractual arrangements and
ineffectual teachers would be corrected or let go if they did not produce for the firm. The school would be able to replace teachers or
hire another firm.

Educational firms could have their own schools like doctors have
hospitals and attorneys have mediation firms. A system of private
for-profit schools would be a much better system than government
schools. The firms would have renewable contracts with local communities to provide the service of educating children. If the firm was
not doing as well as expected the community could contract another
firm. Every child should have the opportunity of going to a good

school and getting the benefit of a good education. The firm could even take responsibility and encourage young people to become part of the firm and even provide scholarships.

There are better ways to instruct children and impart the knowledge required to succeed in the modern world. One is to increase the amount of time spent in school. In the twenty first century, there is no rational reason for months-long summer vacations. It would make more sense to allow parents the option of taking their children out of school for a week or so for family vacations with the proviso that the children study the missed lessons. If religious and cultural holidays were part of the local culture then that would be handled by the local school board or government. Schooling should be considered like a job and lessons are projects to be completed. With more time in school, homework would become a relic as it moves responsibility for teaching away from the school to parents, who themselves may have already spent the day at work.

The number of hours spent in school is similar around the world, about six hours per day of classes. American students spend, on average, about 180 days per year in school while many Asian students about 250. Elsewhere in the world it is somewhere in between. The time spent in school is certainly too short in the United States. Considering the results, it would seem that the Asian child's 250 days per year is much closer to what is needed. Even those Asian students have weekends off plus two weeks of vacation. There should be activities with directed study, community participation and class trips to interesting locations. Students should have some time of their own and the school day would be much more fulfilling.

It is necessary for students to receive a basic education in language and mathematics, but schools should also have specialized classes. There should be schools for the gifted and the special needs students as well as apprenticeship programs. Local governments and private concerns could have scholarships available when a student excels in a particular area or indicates need.

People would do much better in adulthood with skill sets to survive in modern society. Of course, students should be learning communication, math and basic science but there is much more needed for survival in the modern world. It is important to obtain the skills to be good citizens including geography, history, marketing, analyzing current events, government, and politics. Students need to be able to identify advertizing, misinformation and propaganda no matter where it comes from.

All humans and particularly children are susceptible to advertising or propaganda, and it can be difficult to discern the truth from half-truths and fabrication. This lesson would be necessary not just to identify advertizing but more importantly, to prevent despotism that sprouts so easily from government. Students need to understand how government works and when it is not working as it should and particularly when it is getting out of control. They especially need an understanding of their rights as citizens and the limits of the power of government.

In the United States, government schools have a problem teaching what would seem to be extremely important things like how to vote and recognizing and respecting different viewpoints. They avoid discussing things like; what are taxes, where do they go, what the government does with them and how to pay them. There is little to no discussion of anything to do with economics and how to shop. Even more important, create an understanding of banking, credit cards, when and how to obtain a loan or how to start a business.

Students need basic survival skills in an urban environment such as how to do their laundry, cook and prepare meals, be a discerning shopper, get a bus, taxi or how to travel. Again, they must know basic economics and finance, the perils of borrowing, credit / debit cards and how to balance a bank account. They would also need some survival skills if modern conveniences were removed. It may sound strange but all children would be well served having some Boy/Girl Scout knowledge and experience.

All students should have a basic understanding of chemistry, biology and physics. In chemistry, one of the most basics is what is fire, how to start one and put an unwanted one out. There is the relationship of acids, bases and salts. There is the question of what are living things made of, anatomy, genetics and reproduction. There are even more questions that need to be answered. For example, how does gravity hold the Moon and planets in place and how it affects us? Students should learn about atoms and how they combine to form molecules, which are the stuff all things are made of. They would need basic technical skills and understanding modern technology must be part of the curriculum.

Children of all sexes should take "shop" class and learn how find a blown fuse or tripped circuit breaker, fix a lamp and general electrical safety. They need to learn where electricity comes from and how is generated. There should be basic carpentry lessons on how to saw a board, pound a nail, put in a screw and repair drywall. Since we live with them every day, basic auto mechanics and repair would be a wonderful skill to have. Certainly, computer technology, operating systems, Internet searches and simple programming should be included in the curriculum.

Girls and boys should be taught how to maintain personal hygiene. They need to know how to keep themselves clean without removing protective skin oils. Bedding and sleep materials need to be kept fresh to prevent bacteria, mold and insects. There is the importance of maintaining food preparation areas. The washing and maintenance of clothing need to be in the curriculum. Removing waste would include cleaning and recycling and how to prevent mold from forming as well as how to deal with insect and rodent infestations.

One of the greatest inventions that is fundamental to modern healthy living and needs to be understood is water and sanitary systems. There is the knowledge of the distribution of potable water and what a marvel it truly is which may help obviate the incredible pollution of plastic water bottles. Students should know how to repair a faucet and a drain, plus the disposal of biological waste and the operation and repair of toilets. Citizens need to know garbage collection and how it is collected and where it ends up and the necessity of recycling and how it is done.

Many people are not aware of history but only of "popular" culture that is drilled into them by the media and their contemporaries. People around the world and especially Americans have a poor understanding of what came before. The teaching of history in American schools is tedious and there is no "this happened because of that". Teachers are given the task of teaching history from an arbitrary point in the past to another arbitrary time imparting little understanding to their students. In many cases, history in government schools is taught from the government point of view and as such is little different from propaganda.

The components of local and world history, the interconnection of events, people, chronological order plus religion and culture must be taught. The belief systems of other religions are important to understand the peoples of the world. Everyone should know the precepts of all the major religions and their holy days, what they represent and how they are celebrated. They should be learned so that we can understand each other's point of view. They generally have not been taught in the past because of the fear that some students would see something better and convert. This is still true in areas with fundamentalist religions.

There is no question that language unites people and the teaching of another language is an absolute must not only for cultural reasons but also for practical reasons. The Americas is one of the unique places in the world where the tide of history has left only a few dominant languages. One can travel from above the Arctic Circle to Tierra del Fuego at the tip of South America and speak to almost anyone as a first or second language in English or Spanish. Both of those languages have many common historical roots from the original

Indo-European as well as Latin and Greek and it is comparatively easy for each to learn the other, as there are many points of contact. It would be a shame that they are not required for all students in the Americas.

Peoples in other parts of the world generally learn a second language that will help them with every day situation. Many, especially those who have traveled a bit, can get by in at least one other language. There are the languages of the larger world that are important to be learned such as Mandarin, Hindi, Arabic, Cantonese, Portuguese, and Russian. Bahasa Indonesia is one of the easiest natural languages to learn but with less than 25 million first language speakers it is one of the smallest. Linguistics or the study of language and all languages as structures of written words, sounds and meanings should most certainly be taught as an introduction into critical thinking.

A single language that is easy to learn, such as Esperanto or Globish, should be taught to all students. They are especially easy for the interrelated European language speakers to learn. Esperanto can be learned five times faster than a natural language because of the simple grammar and common words. It is, by far, the largest artificial language. Polish scholar Leyzer Zamengov thought that if people could speak to each other there would be less conflict. He derived it from mostly from the Indo-European language group that includes more than half the population of the world. Even students from non-Latin based alphabet areas will have little problem, especially because pronunciation is invariant and similar to the widely spoken Spanish.

Globish is actually English but as its developer, Frenchman Jean-Paul Nerriere, says; it is free from the English or American culture. It has no idioms, jokes and a simple sentence structure. It uses only 1500 words, many of which are international, such as police and taxi. People from around the world who have had some lessons or have been exposed to English will find it easy and can pick it up in few weeks. People will be able to communicate to both native and non-native English speakers. English is the most common language on the Internet and there would be an easier exchange of information. It is not a bias toward English; it takes advantage of the fact that English is the most widespread first and second language in the world. Unfortunately, with Esperanto, you can speak with two million other Esperantists, but with Globish, you can reach the billions of people that already speak English as a first or second language.

Another problem related to education is that there is far too little money spent on research and development, which should be an industry in its own right. The collection and collating of knowledge is one of the most important endeavors of humankind. Pundits complain about some seemingly silly studies but there is no knowledge that should not be obtained. All knowledge should be studied, codified and restudied constantly teasing every bit of information.

There should be private enterprise research organizations whose primary goal is to create ideas, to produce patents. The manufacturing, marketing and other organizations would contract a research organization to produce a workable idea. The research company could also independently produce ideas for sale or lease. The research company could be a stand-alone organization or be part of a corporation or an academic institution. The organization would be large enough to protect themselves and their researchers from patent theft. It must be worthwhile to the research organization so the knowledge obtained should be patentable for a period of time. It must be large enough to be able to prevent large corporations and law firms from stealing the patents by threatening expensive litigation. There are patents for new inventions and ideas but it is not always certain that they are useful. There should be trial period made available at a lower cost for market research.

Individuals and groups with an idea, completed or needing development, could go to one of these companies that would review the idea. There would be different research companies in different areas of endeavor so that one would know where to start. It would be similar to finding a publisher for a book. If there were an idea for a new electronic gadget, then one would go to companies that specialize in electronics. The same goes for drugs and medical procedures. There times when something should be studied but there is no available funding. The individual or group could go to other organizations that would altruistically fund the project much as it is done now.

If the government is to instigate some research, there must be checks and balances because of the tendency to corruption and misuse of public money. It must also have a clear goal that it would not place a burden on taxpayers unless there is a guaranteed return on the investment. It would include research into such things as lowering the cost of drugs and medical treatments as well as subsidies to educational institutions that would actually lower tuition costs.

There are so few scientists, engineers and technicians, more people must become involved. If more people were educated in engineering and sciences, they would not only enrich themselves but all of humanity. Technology would advance much faster with more minds and money working on problems. The goal of education should be to produce these people so that they will be confident in their abilities but tempered with ethics.

The majority of humanity is not permitted to lift their eyes from the dirt. They are the tools of the elites, cannon fodder for wars. Their primary concerns are survival and procreation but they are capable of so much more. We must educate people with the truth, history and the sciences so they can then be truly free to form their own thoughts. Education would enrich all of humanity and would provide the human capital to progress humanity from a single planet.

Energy

Reason and justice tell me there's more love for humanity in electricity and steam than in chastity and
vegetarianism.

~ANTON CHEKHOV 1882

ANYTHING THAT IS possible can be done with enough energy;
things can be built and maintained, any place can become habitable.
Inexpensive energy can make the challenging, achievable. It can put
people to work, grow food, improve health and quality of life as well
as modernize nations. Modern civilization depends upon electrical
energy because the convenience is difficult to beat. All you have to
do is flip a switch and you have light, heat, cooling and even the distribution of data, pictures and sounds from around town and far away
lands. The electrical distribution infrastructure is relatively inexpensive, compared to other energy distribution systems.

In large scale electrical generation and distribution there are two
basic types of generators, base power and peak power. These power
plants are interconnected in huge regional grids so if one plant goes
off line others will take over the load. The load is all the industry and
households connected to and take power from the grid. Base power

is generated to produce the minimum amount needed by the power grid. It is usually powered by coal, hydro, gas or nuclear energy. An average size coal, gas or nuclear base power plant will produce about eight terawatt-hours of electrical energy per year.

Base power generators are designed to provide a great deal of inexpensive power. It is done by keeping output constant over a long period of time so that fuel costs can be anticipated. Hydroelectric power is used for base power generation because after the huge expense of construction of the dam is considered there are no fuel costs, only the cost of maintenance. Almost all major rivers in the world are dammed to generate electricity and, ostensibly, to control flooding. Needless to say, the damming of rivers has a huge environmental cost.

Coal is an inexpensive fuel source, used since ancient times, that provides almost half of the electrical power in the United States and the majority of power in China and the world. It is plentiful, but it is almost pure carbon that is burned with oxygen from the atmosphere producing carbon dioxide. Much of the coal in the world contains impurities, usually sulfurous compounds. When used for electrical production, it has to be ground into a fine powder to be burned efficiently. There are scrubbing technologies that can remove the carbon dioxide and the much more noxious sulfur dioxide, which causes acid rain. Scrubbing is done to prevent pollutants from being released into the atmosphere but it does use more energy and adds to the cost.

Another commonly used fuel is natural gas from oil and gas wells and produces almost one quarter of the electricity in the US. The advantage of natural gas over coal is that it contains hydrogen as well as carbon so when it is burned it makes water as well as carbon dioxide. In addition, because it is a gas it does not have to be powdered to use. It and other fuels, such as coal, geothermal, gas and nuclear are used to create high-pressure steam that drives a steam turbine. The spinning turbine rotates a generator to produce electricity.

Prime Minister Pierre Messmer and the nation of France, poor in energy resources, made the decision in 1974 to go nuclear. They built an atomic power network around the country that now provides almost eighty percent of French electricity as well as a nice profit selling the remainder around the rest of Europe. There have been incidents, but there has never been a radiation related death in the French power system. France has one-tenth the carbon dioxide footprint (carbon-based fuel used) of the more populous Germany and one third of tiny Denmark, which has no nuclear power plants.

Peak power, as the name implies, is needed when the demand for power increases beyond base power. This is what happens on a hotter or colder than normal day or when people return home from work and school and dinner preparation begins and such things as air conditioners, heaters and stoves are turned on. Demand for electricity quickly increases. If there were no peak power generation there would be brownouts and outages as the voltage dipped due to changing conditions. Peak power generators must be fast turn-on to be quickly added to the supply. They are usually driven by gas turbines, which are basically jet engines with an electrical generator attached. Diesel engines are also commonly used.

Modern society could not exist without inexpensive energy. Sadly, there are many energy frauds being perpetrated by the unscrupulous. They usually involve propaganda that identifies a problem such as "Global Warming" or "Climate Change" then to come up with a "solution". The solution always involves higher prices, more taxes and more government control. There are many, many examples of this in action. We are told what we must do to "save the planet" from ourselves but how much of this is true and how much is propaganda?

The majority of the sunlight that hits the Earth evaporates water from the Oceans and combined with the Earth's rotation creates weather. All of the photosynthetic plants and cyanobacteria on the earth use about one percent of the solar energy that strikes the earth's surface. The total energy consumed by all human activities is about one percent of that. Humanity is responsible for less than three parts in one thousand of carbon dioxide production. A single volcano will produce more carbon dioxide that all the machinations of humanity. Nevertheless, let's take the hyperbole seriously for a moment and see where it goes with "ecological" energy systems.

How about wind turbines to generate electric power? One would think from the all the propaganda that they should be like hydro-electric dams but using the winds instead of water and create no pollution. The problem is they only make electricity when the wind is blowing and in a narrow range of wind speed. The power in the wind varies as the cube of the velocity so turbines are designed for a particular wind velocity. If the speed is halved, the power output drops to almost one tenth. If the speed is doubled it will tear itself apart. They do not generate if there is not enough wind or there is too much.

If there were a large number of turbines over a large area, it could be designed to average out. Nevertheless, how large does it have to be? A large group of wind turbines is called a "farm" presumably because from far away they would look like a field of flowers. A farm of wind turbines numbering over ten thousand units would be needed to produce the same power output as the average coal or nuclear power plant. Each wind turbine, to be the most efficient, should be spaced at least one kilometer from the next. A wind farm that could produce eight terawatt-hours per year would need an area the size of Washington, DC or Lichtenstein. Even with this size, it would replace only one conventional power plant.

There are dirty secrets about wind turbines that are not advertised, such as they require a great deal of maintenance, they are noisy and kill many birds and even more bats. The tips of the blades move fast, more than three hundred kilometers per hour. Birds can't see them and half a million are killed per year in the United States alone. Bats are killed in the millions, when they get too close the air pressure differential sucks their lungs out. If bats and birds don't eat the insects, farmers must use more pesticide, which ends up in our food.

Another dirty secret about wind turbines is that down there, on the ground, next to the piles of dead birds and bats there usually is a small building. In the building is a diesel generator providing power when the wind isn't blowing properly. There are only certain areas of the world where there is enough energy in the wind to be harvested commercially. There are even fewer locations where the need is close and the electricity does not have to be transmitted long distances. Wind turbines are, nevertheless, ideal for their historic use, which is pumping water using less efficient turbines.

My wife and I went to visit a German built wind turbine at Swaffham in eastern England. It had an observation gondola below the propeller nacelle. It was impressive and quite a thrill for the tourists. It would rock back and forth as the giant blades went across your field of view. It has shut down since then. It is quite sad and if it was so wonderful and for all the money that the fine English folks paid for it, why was it closed after only a few years? The answer is, the cost of operation had far exceeded that of the local coal and nuclear power plants. It was nothing more than a big costly toy and a propaganda tool. It also had the little blockhouse at the base with the diesel generator.

Surely, solar power plants in hot desert areas must be the ticket in renewable energy; the Sun will be there every day. Unfortunately, they have the problem that you would need a quite number of them to make a reasonable amount of power. Worse, they only work half the time because they don't collect any power at night. Sunlight is attenuated by the atmosphere, clouds and any dust on the unit so they have to be kept clean. Since the mirrors must be located in a dusty desert they require constant cleaning greatly increasing the operating cost.

Generators that collect energy directly from the Sun come in two varieties, photovoltaic and thermal. Photovoltaic solar panels convert sunlight directly into electricity. They work much better in raw sunlight in space or on the Moon without the filter of Earth's atmosphere. On the Earth, photovoltaic panels are excellent to power small electronics in remote locations where there is adequate sunlight. There was a plan for solar power stations in Earth orbit but it was not approved by the United States Congress.

Large solar power plants that use thermal energy collectors have an array of Sun tracking mirrors reflecting sunlight to focus it on a collection area, generally made of salt with embedded pipes. The energy is used to heat water into steam that is then used in conventional turbines similar to those used in coal or nuclear plants. One of the world's largest solar power generators is the Solar Energy Generating System (SEGS) in the California Mojave desert. It is the area that receives the most sunlight of anywhere in the United States. There are a million tracking collection mirrors that follow the Sun across the sky located over six square kilometers. The SEGS plants have an average production of one quarter of a terawatt-hour per year. It sounds like a great deal but it is only about three percent of the average conventional base power plant.

To build a solar power plant large enough to produce the power output that an average base power plant produces, would require a mirror field larger than Washington, DC. A solar power plant this large would replace only one of the thousands of electrical power plants in the United States. There is a dirty little secret here too; to feed the electrical grid at night the turbines use steam from burning natural gas. In 1999, at SEGS, a tank of therminol exploded sending flames into the sky and a million gallons of poisonous poly-biphenyl (PCB's) into the environment. Solar power plants, even the small facilities that exist, kill birds and bats in the tens of thousands. They are called "streamers" by the workers because they burst into flames as they pass thru the superhot beam of heat and light.

The amount of power garnered from all wind and solar power plants that is added to worldwide power grids, after a more than half a century of development, is statistically next to nothing. If they were not heavily subsidized by governments and yet another pocket for taxpayer dollars to disappear into, they would not be even be considered as viable alternatives. The spending and propaganda continues unabated with no investigation by the so-called government watchdogs in the popular media.

A green plant could be thought of as a machine that converts sunlight into storable energy. How about ethanol, a fuel distilled from plant sugar fermentation? It has to be a great idea converting corn or other plant material into motor fuel. A natural process, plants are self-cleaning and repairing and they aim themselves toward the Sun as well as stabilize the atmosphere. Sustainable energy from biofuels or biologically produced fuel is a lovely idea. One can harvest plant material and convert it to a more convenient fuel, such as alcohol. The fuel would then be burned in modern engines. The oxidized fuel would be returned to the atmosphere as carbon dioxide and the water to the Earth.

Biofuel is a beautiful idea, if it were far more efficient and actually sustainable. In general, it takes about ten times as much energy to produce a quantity of plant matter than can be extracted from the plant. It is interesting to note that some in the government and the "environmental" industry would have you believe that this equation can be turned around to produce energy from plants. The beautiful dream becomes even more of a nightmare when the inefficiencies of chemical conversion are considered. Ethanol production requires vast amounts of land that was previously wild or used to produce food and even vaster amounts of fresh water as well as expensive fertilizer.

In the United States a huge amount of ethanol is made from corn and added to gasoline. It not only lowers the distance the vehicle can travel per liter of fuel but it is also subsidized by taxpayers. Corn has become considerably more expensive. It has increased so much that many Latin Americans had to switch to tacos made from wheat and other flours. It is difficult for a poor family to compete with a subsidized industry that gets "free" money from the government. Corn is used by the agricultural industry as animal feed and many processed foods. The high price of corn caused a general increase in the price of food. Ethanol would not be a viable industry if it were not heavily dependant on taxpayer money and is just more governmental dishonesty.

When energy is removed from the environment it affects the environment in unpredictable ways and the ecosystem. "Green energy" is, in fact, worse than coal and oil. There are energy sources that are not extracted from the ecosystem and are consequently much less damaging to the environment than the so-called green alternatives.

There is nuclear fusion reactor technology where reactions similar to the Sun can be used to generate sustainable power. The goal is to increase the density and temperature of hydrogen to cause it to fuse into helium. It has been done but the process has not produced enough energy, considering the required investment, to be used commercially. It is an energy source with great promise that has yet to deliver after a half century of research. It would be nonpolluting because there is little actual matter involved, and that is mostly hydrogen isotopes extracted at great cost from seawater.

The latest fusion project, located in southern France, is the ITER or International Thermonuclear Reactor, a consortium of many nations. It is a Soviet design Tokomak type of reactor, using magnetic fields to squeeze hydrogen isotopes to a high density. Much money has been spent and there is still a great deal of engineering to be done. It is a long way from using the extremely plentiful hydrogen or even the rare hydrogen isotopes found in the ocean. Even using exotic hydrogen isotopes like deuterium and tritium testing is not to begin until 2027 and full-scale operation may be yet another half century away.

There are other "green" power generation schemes but they suffer from similar problems. Concentrating and extracting power on an industrial scale from the environment will cause more damage to the environment than more conventional systems. One system is geothermal or extracting power from the internal heat of the earth. It has few disadvantages other than they have to be built in volcanically active areas.

The only originally government supported alternate energy that seems to have worked out well is the much maligned nuclear power. Nuclear power is more than a million times more powerful than carbon fuel; one kilogram of enriched uranium is almost equal to two thousand tons of coal. Once it was shown that power could be extracted from nuclear fission in the basement of the University of Chicago in 1942, the nuclear industry took off.

Unfortunately, most atomic research was to build bombs. Nevertheless, it was shown to be safe if handled properly. Since so much power was concentrated in a smaller volume, it makes perfect sense that care would need to be taken. Uranium power plants would be much more viable in the United States if the Democratic Party had allowed the construction of the Yucca Mountain nuclear waste repository. The highly radioactive waste products are instead stored in barrels on site at the many nuclear power stations. Perhaps, it would have not been needed, as it sorely is now, if a different direction had been taken.

Power

I was actually telling people that - by harnessing the atom - we could enter a new era of unlimited power that would do away with the need to dam our beautiful streams.

~David R. Brower

THERE ARE VIABLE low-pollution, high-energy sources that have been developed but not funded and exploited to the extent that they should be. Several come to mind that are well within current technology that are not commonly used. Is it because they are expensive and with unknown harm to the environment? Perhaps, there are reasons that are more sinister. It is the most readily available source of actually green energy that produces very little pollutants and has the smallest effect on the environment.

Thorium! Never heard of it? It is an ideal fuel for atomic reactors because it cannot maintain a reaction without feedback and if unattended it would stop by itself. Thorium is a natural radioactive element that is similar to but far less dangerous than uranium and far more abundant. In fact, it is as common as lead. The Thorium Energy

Alliance says that there is enough in the United States to power the entire country at its current level for the next several thousand years.

Because thorium is more abundant than uranium, mining it is much less damaging to the environment. It requires less processing than uranium; these and other reasons make it much less expensive. Thorium reactors have little radioactive waste compared to uranium reactors and if used the Yucca Mountain repository would not be necessary as it is with uranium reactors. Thorium produces about a thousand times less waste from the mine all the way to the reactor than uranium. Most existing uranium reactors can be converted to the use of thorium.

There are many more reasons to use thorium reactors including the fact that they are much less expensive to build than other power sources. There is a technology called Liquid Salt Thorium Reactor or LFTR that is extremely safe for use just about anywhere. It does not require a massive containment facility and it does not emit dangerous gamma rays as uranium does. Shipping thorium has none of the danger of uranium and its deadly waste products. Thorium has been considered a waste product of mining rare earth metals. In fact, there are several thousand tons, equivalent to millions of tons of coal, buried in a shallow grave in Nevada.

Small thorium reactors have been developed that can inexpensively power a town or a vehicle as large as an ocean liner or as small as an automobile. These power plants could be networked over a wide area to provide constant electricity without transmission loss and without the security needed for uranium reactors. The reaction vessel would be in a sealed steel container delivered to site on a rail car or the back of a semitrailer. When the fuel has been expended in a decade or so another reaction vessel is delivered to replace the spent one. The spent vessel would return to the factory to be recharged. This system is not being used in the United States because of irrational fear of fissionable fuels created by propaganda as well as governmental policies.

The major reason why thorium has not been used for energy production is that it is cannot be used to make weapons. Very simply, it will not go boom. In 1997 the International Scientific Symposium on Nuclear Fuel Cycles concluded that the primary reason thorium had not been commonly used in reactors is that there are no fissile isotopes. It is unfortunate that the bad publicity about uranium reactors has poisoned the waters for thorium reactors.

Recently, much of the nuclear power generated in the United States has come from uranium purchased from Russia that originated in disassembled Soviet nuclear ballistic missiles. The application of uranium, instead of thorium, in generating electrical power for the last half century is, at best, homicidal insanity. There is a much safer, cheaper alternative. It seems that governments want to have us dependant upon carbon fuels while they make end of the world bombs.

China is developing thorium reactors because of its investment in rare earths. Germany has had the first power plant that does not use uranium as a fuel. India, which has one fourth of the world's thorium, is also building thorium reactor power stations. The largest reserves are located in India, Canada, South Africa, Brazil and the United States. Unfortunately, the Obama administration has announced another eight billion in loan guarantees for more uranium reactors.

Inexpensive electricity from Thorium reactors could be used to power electric high-speed rail systems as they exist currently in most of Europe, Japan and China. It can desalinate water in arid areas and provide power in remote areas. In fact, they can be used to colonize parts of the world that are considered too extreme for habitation on the Earth. Cheap energy, albeit from oil, has turned hot sweaty Dubai into an international trading location and vacation wonderland. Thorium would open up the vast frozen areas including Siberia, Antarctica, Greenland and the Canadian North. There are also the great desert areas that can be made green with desalinated water.

The areas with harsh climates that add up to the majority of the land surface of the Earth could have farms, cities and more productive habitats instead of barren land.

Fusion power converts hydrogen isotopes into energy, which is the same as powers the sun and all the stars. Nuclear fusion is a dream that is always 30 years away. Safe energy from Thorium reactors is here and now. Cheap energy from thorium would allow dams for generating electricity to be destroyed and rivers to run naturally. Thorium warms the Earth as half of the energy to keep the core molten is from radioactivity musty thorium. It will serve humankind for many years to come.

Now then, how about non-polluting devices, perhaps they can "save" us from a hypothetical global warming? Hydrogen powered cars, what a wonderful idea! They would burn pure hydrogen in an internal combustion engine or a fuel cell reaction chamber. In both cases, the hydrogen would combine with oxygen in the atmosphere and produce nothing more than pure water. You may have seen demonstrations on television showing someone holding a glass under the automobile exhaust and drinking the emissions. Where is the problem? What is not told? Oh, wait... where does the hydrogen come from?

Pure hydrogen is commercially produced in several ways. One method is to "crack" water into its components hydrogen and oxygen using electrical energy. It requires a great deal of electrical energy and the process is quite inefficient. One has to consider where the fuel comes from to make the electricity. In the United States and most other places in the world, it will probably be from coal powered electric generators. Another method to create hydrogen is to burn coal with hot steam. The carbon grabs the oxygen from the water and releases hydrogen and you are left with a lot of carbon dioxide and a lot of waste heat. A hydrogen-powered car is really an inefficient coal powered car. It would be far more efficient to burn the coal in the vehicle in the first place.

Battery powered electric cars are yet another inefficient system that borders on being, dare I say... a scam. The electricity is not magically created on site; it comes from a far away electric power plant that uses, again in most of the world, coal. The power grids that provide electrical power are high voltage alternating current but batteries use low voltage direct current, a conversion that further reduces systemic efficiency. Battery technology has long been the problem for electric vehicles, the power density and charging speed is not good enough.

A solution to the problems of batteries is the high-density capacitor as it has a fast charge time. A capacitor uses the electrical stress across an insulator to hold the charge unlike the battery that uses chemical reactions to charge and discharge. The battery will eventually wear out while the capacitor will not. There is still a lot of research and the result will probably be a battery – capacitor hybrid to store the energy from the base power plant. Nevertheless, like hydrogen power, the system is still being powered by coal.

Then again, a small electrically powered low speed surrey would be an efficient way to travel around a community especially if it were recharged by a solar panel on the roof. It would work especially well in hot dry places around the world. It would not look like a Tesla or even a Volt automobile it would look more like an old horse drawn carriage without the horse. It could even have pedals like a bicycle to supplement the batteries. The power plant would be perhaps a one to five kilowatt motor with a maximum speed of forty kilometers per hour. It would be a non-polluting solution in city area. Unfortunately, it would not work for long commutes but that issue could be solved by rapid transit systems.

The single advantage of hydrogen and electric vehicles over hydrocarbon fuels is that pollution is not created where the vehicle is, but where the energy conversion is made. To avoid local pollution, the state of California has made a commitment to electric vehicles but has also made the bizarre decision to make it difficult to generate power where it is needed. The cost of electricity on the West Coast of the United States has skyrocketed and is now the most expensive in the United States. The smoke from the burning coal that makes the electricity is not in Beverly Hills but over the border in Arizona. There has to be even more coal burned to compensate for transmission loss. The infrastructure problems of Southern California could be solved by a network of Thorium power plants, desalination plants and a common sense immigration policy.

One form of energy storage that has been neglected of late for transportation is compressed air. It is the same stuff that can be heard in auto repair shops driving tools and driving nails at construction sites. In the late Nineteenth and early Twentieth century, before the widespread use of electricity, compressed air was used as a portable source of energy. Fireless locomotives have been used in mines, trams and as "donkeys" in rail yards. It is certainly not a new concept. Even today, ten percent of the electrical energy produced is used for air compression.

There have been many compressed air automobiles developed but have not had the popularity of liquid fueled automobiles because of the shorter range. The biggest advantage of compressed air is its availability; it is all around us. The second big advantage is that is would allow fast recharging. An automobile would pull up to the charging station and the hose clamped onto the vehicle's inlet valve and "Psst"... in a few moments, it is now charged. The charging station can be a business or it could be in the home.

The problem with compressed air has been the storage capacity and the danger of an exploding steel tank from either corrosion or a collision. The tank problem has been solved by using high pressure in an extremely strong carbon fiber tank. The tank would have a seam and since carbon fiber is a fabric, instead of shattering like a steel tank, it would rip open. It would release the pressure much slower and cause much less damage. The seam is the weakest part of the tank so instead of exploding under stress it will tear along the seam like an old pair of pants.

A hybrid compressed air and gasoline automobile would be similar in operation to a hybrid electric. Air tanks would store energy without the cost and environmental issues from replacing and recycling batteries. Compressed air motors are smaller, lighter and more powerful than gasoline or electric motors. If built properly, it would not be affected by water and could be used in any sort of watercraft. Compressed air engines with carbon fiber tanks could even be made light enough to power an aircraft, especially with highly compressed liquid air.

In personal transportation systems, it is difficult to surpass the advantages of liquid fuels such as gasoline, kerosene and especially diesel fuel. They have a much higher energy density than batteries, about one hundred times as much energy per unit volume as a lead battery. It is the most inexpensive and safe way to store energy for portable use. Liquid fuels can be safely handled by even the most maladroit individual. It is much easier to fill a tank with liquid fuel than handling a compressed gas that must be secured and have an airtight connection. There are so many things that can go wrong with high-pressure gases; even compressed air can be dangerous for unskilled operators. It is especially true with flammable gases, including hydrogen, natural gas, propane, etc. High-pressure gas systems should be left to the professionals.

Liquids are easier to handle than using a large electrical plug. Using inexpensive thorium power, high energy liquid fuels can be made from coal or even carbon dioxide and water, the ultimate non-polluter. A small local nuclear power plant could make liquid fuel and other portable energies such as hydrogen, battery and compressed air as viable substitutes for fossil fuels as needed.

Thorium reactors are current technology and could serve humanity for many centuries but the ultimate source of power would be the Sun itself in the form of solar power collectors. On the surface of the Earth, solar power is too inconsistent and diluted. Lunar colonies would have them conveniently on the surface of the moon or in orbit. The Earth would have them in geosynchronous orbit orbiting above a fixed point above the equator. They would collect power from the Sun with huge solar photovoltaic panels, a proven technology already in use for communications satellites. The power generated in space would be sent to the Earth on beams of microwaves and received on antenna farms. The farms would need to be fairly large so that the power beam is not deadly to flying animals or aircraft.

There are more technologies that can be used in space to extract energy from such things as the solar wind. A power generator in an obit close to the Sun could have a conducting tether extended a kilometer or more. The voltage difference from the induced electricity would capture large amounts of energy. These devices could capture billions times as much power as all human civilization presently consumes. Using microwave beams and lasers, it could not only be sent to power planetary-based civilizations but also power thousands of spacecraft for speedy travel around the solar system and even to other stars.

The ultimate portable fuel given the current extent of human knowledge is antimatter; it is the opposite of matter. When an atom of the ordinary stuff around us meets an anti-atom, they combine in the ultimate burst of energy. Bang! The matter and antimatter combination demonstrates Einstein's famous "$E=mc2$" equation. The matter and antimatter are completely annihilated and converted to energy. Since matter cannot be use to contain antimatter, magnetic "bottles" or electrical fields are used. It has a huge potential to store energy, a single gram of antimatter has about the same energy as ten thousand tons of coal. It has an energy density ten billion times as much as gasoline.

Currently, only minute quantities of antimatter are made in laboratories. Once the methods are perfected, factories in solar orbit using the energy of the Sun could make much larger quantities and lower the price. The Sun also creates some antimatter in solar flares that could be captured and concentrated. A factory in orbit a safe ten million kilometers from the sun can collect about two hundred times as the energy that is available in Earth orbit. Energy does not have to be a problem, it is the solution.

Avarice

When plunder becomes a way of life for a group of
men living together in society, they create for themselves, in the course of time, a legal system that
authorizes it and a moral code that glorifies it.

~FREDERIC BASTAIT

WE CAN SEE from history and current events what the international banking monopolies have been doing with their cronies in the
government. They are enriching themselves with what are little more
than paper games; fraud and overcomplicated financial "products". It
is really nothing more than high stakes gambling and worse, the game
is rigged. They work tirelessly to increase their power and control to
protect their holdings. In many ways, they are at the root cause of
poverty and wars. Greed is not a bad thing, in fact, it drives people to
better themselves but it can be a psychosis when the acquisition of
wealth becomes the goal in itself.

One has to reflect on how this state of affairs came to be. The present world economic system evolved from the moneylenders in the
European Middle Ages. Christians were not allowed, by the church,
to lend money because of misunderstood scriptural restrictions on

usury. Coins were in use but in large numbers were heavy and could be easily stolen. Because of this, Jewish moneylenders kept precious metal coins in a safe place and used written notes representing them, which became a de facto currency.

Moneylenders formed networks of trust that allowed for the flow of value from one area to another. Gold, for example, could be given to a lender in one town and a note carried to a second lender in another town who would release gold of the same value to the holder of the note. Other parts of the world such as China and the Middle East had similar systems but without the religious segregation. These notes are commodity-backed money and are called promissory notes or banknotes. Commodity backed money can be redeemed for something that has intrinsic value. Paper money that was issued in the United States until 1963 was silver certificates and, in principal, could be redeemed as such.

The medieval system of European banking houses made a profit by lending out money put in by depositors. In many cases, the royal and / or powerful families, so they would not have to dirty their hands, would lend their wealth to the moneylenders. It would become a two way street but was dangerous to be caught cheating them. The moneylenders would make loans to businesses but would charge high interest. It was because there was so much risk of default and money had to be paid on demand to the depositors. Borrowers would have to pay high interest rates in the range of thirty to fifty percent and they had to have collateral. If the borrower defaulted on the loan, the lender would assume ownership of the collateral. This system worked for many centuries into modern times and moneylenders themselves became rich and powerful.

Making loans to the aristocracy would always be problematic because then as now they make the rules. They were also the source of anti-Semitism when they were debtors. They could denounce the lender's religious practices as being an affront to the local religion. It was actually all about money and not religion. There were many cases where Jewish lenders and any other Jews were murdered or deported because of an unscrupulous aristocracy who owed them money.

Moneylenders would form into groups for mutual protection that created the large banking houses. A Frankfurter moneylender in the 18th century by the name of Rothschild had five sons. He sent these sons to the centers of population and wealth around Europe. Because they could trust each other, the family became the center of international finance and they are still a powerful organization to this day.

The governments of the day always had treasuries to store the wealth of the aristocracy, but when they noticed the power and profit of the moneylenders, they took over the task of maintaining the medium of exchange. National banks were created and like the moneylenders would issue representative currency. It also carried the promise to pay the bearer something of actual value on demand such as silver or gold. This money in the past was actually redeemable for precious metal coin of equal value. The Chinese were the first to use paper to replace a commodity but conversion to actual metal was rarely allowed. Marco Polo wrote of his travels in China "All these pieces of paper are issued with as much solemnity and authority as if they were of pure gold or silver."

Some in the banking industry and government realized that otherwise worthless paper could be given value if the government forced everyone to accept it. It is called fiat currency or money by decree. Fiat money is created when the government orders that a piece of paper have more value, usually far more, than the paper itself. Currency around the world, in its modern form, is a fancy printed piece of paper without even a promise of value. The government also makes laws that say no other currency is allowed so what is issued is the only recourse. Government issued currency is given some value by the ability to use it to pay taxes.

A major problem is there is no restraint on amount of fiat currency that can be created by simply printing it, or now as digits added to computerized accounts. When more fiat money is added to circulation, the additional money is chasing the same goods and services, which inflates their cost. As prices increase, it effectively reduces the value of incomes, savings and retirement programs. The major problem with fiat currency because it has no intrinsic value, is that it is allowed to lose value with time. When currency losses value the cost of commodities increases or inflate. At the same time interest payments on loans become less valuable when compared to a commodity such as silver. This process makes it easier for governments to pay interest on debts, especially if taxes are also constantly increasing. Considering how it works, inflation is actually a stealth tax that government imposes on the holders of the fiat currency.

The crisis of modern finance is what was once considered immoral and illegal and that is fractional banking. In earlier times, money was not lent without considerable collateral because the bank needed to have something to back the loan. In the case of default, there had to be something of value deposited in the vault or immovable like real estate. Fractional banking allows the banks to lend out more money than it has in deposits, much more.

In fractional banking, the ratio of the deposits to the amount of money that can be loaned out is called the liquidity ratio. This ratio, for example, allows that for every dollar in the vault seven can be loaned out. In the United States even this rule has been dropped. To put it another way, the bank need not have any assets. When it makes a loan, it is creating money from nothing. Banks even "lend" each other money creating "assets" out of thin air without producing anything.

Fractional banking allows the bank to lend what is actually imaginary money. It is easier for borrowers to obtain unsecured loans because the bank has no risk. In many cases, there is no collateral required for these loans and they are a high risk of default. The banks also charge high interest on these loans and credit cards, which are actually unsecured loans. It is certainly a sweet deal for the banks getting interest on imaginary money and selling loan products on money they do not have. The large-scale wars of the Twentieth Century could not have happened without the vast sums created from nothing by fractional banking.

A situation is created where a bank that requires collateral can be put out of business by one that does not. This is exactly what has happened in the United States and many other places around the world and why there are so many small bank "failures", they cannot compete with the big banks unfair tactics. That is what is going on now; there are only a few large banks, "too big to fail", that have interests everywhere. Since there are few limits on how much a bank can lend, depositors become unimportant which is why there are now charges for checking accounts, minimum account balances and penalties. That is, you now have to pay the bank to "store" your money.

One of the more important concepts in finance is the "velocity of money" or how fast it changes hands. If you have one hundred dollars in a shoebox under the bed, it has no impact upon the economy because it is not doing anything. However, if one has a ten-dollar bill that is used to buy food, the grocery then pays the clerk who then buys a gasoline and so on. If that ten-dollar bill changes hands ten times in a day, it does the job of a hundred dollars. If it changes hands a hundred times a month it acts like a thousand dollars. The faster money changes hands per unit of time the more money it seems that there is in circulation. The best indication of an advancing economy is money circulating rapidly. Money becomes valuable and the currency and the economy is strong.

As imaginary money is added to the economy by fractional banking, it appears as tho the velocity of money is increasing. In fact, the opposite is happening. The value of money itself is decreasing causing the price of goods and services to increase or inflate. We have entered the age where money is nothing more than numbers in a computer. Transactions are carried out between computers, extracting taxes and user fees automatically with every exchange.

Governments and banks can "create" more money by simply adding it to the digital ledger. In modern countries, credit cards and debt are now more common than cash. Governments even distribute welfare payments by debit cards. That data in those computers is "money" and is still fiat but has even less intrinsic value than a piece of paper. Using fiat money and fractional banking, governments, corporations and private citizens have taken upon huge debt loads.

Interest on secured loans such as real estate can be comparatively low; the interest on savings deposits is even lower. Because of fractional banking, there is constant inflation that further lowers the value of those savings accounts. Even the pitiful interest accrued on those accounts is then taxed. These factors discourage putting money into savings accounts but incentivizes borrowing and going into debt. Saving for retirement is now a thing of the past, one must "invest" money for retirement and that barely keeps up with inflation.

In the Twentieth Century consortiums of international banks, such as the United States Federal Reserve or the "Fed" were formed allegedly to prevent panics and stabilize the stock market. It is not a government agency at all but a consortium of its member banks, many international. It was given the power by Congress to maintain the medium of exchange, the dollar.

Simplistically, the Federal Reserve decides when the United States "needs more money". It then prints it or in the modern version adds digits to the computers at the member banks. There are complex paper games between the Fed, its member banks, and the United States Treasury. The member banks ultimately benefit from these games and use the money to pay huge dividends to their officers or lend to preferred groups for even more leverage.

To add injury to insult this imaginary money is "borrowed" by the United States Treasury. The Federal Reserve also prints treasury notes or treasuries that are sold as "safe" investments. The treasuries are loan instruments that require interest be paid on them. The treasuries are monetized by the Fed, which means that they just keep them on the books. The government is not required to pay the debt; it uses taxpayer money to pay the interest, which adds up year after year. This interest has now become a significant part of the United States Federal budget. It is these loans by the Fed of imaginary money that pays the difference between revenue and spending or since there has never been a surplus, the deficit.

There is the usual propaganda that says there have been surpluses from time to time in American history, such as that attributed to President Bill Clinton. In reality, the United States maintains an ever-increasing permanent yearly debt, which in 2013 totals approximately seventeen trillion dollars. The deficit for the last few years has been well over a trillion dollars every year that is added to the debt. During the Clinton administration, the national debt was over five trillion dollars. Worse, if a private citizen wanted to obtain a loan all of their commitments or liabilities would be taken into account. It is not true for governments. There are long-term commitments or spending that is mandated by laws made by irresponsible politicians and the negligent voters that keep them in power.

There are two types of spending by the United States Federal Government, discretionary and mandatory which over the years seem to have reversed priorities. Discretionary spending can be changed by the regime in power but mandatory cannot be changed without changing the law. Discretionary spending includes such things as the military, science foundation, NASA, civil engineering works, National Institute of Health and even the Justice Department. Mandatory spending includes such things as Federal welfare programs. It also includes interest on the debt, which amounted to over two and a half trillion dollars in 2013.

There are unfunded liabilities that have to be paid. There is no lockbox, as was alluded to by Vice President Al Gore, Social Security is bankrupt and is paid out of current revenue. The same goes for Medicare, Medicaid and now the ACA or "Obamacare". They increase as more and more people retire or become old and ill or poverty-stricken. These mandatory spending items can be projected so that the actual current United States Federal liability is over two hundred trillion dollars in 2013. Children, before they are even born, are responsible for this astronomical public debt. Personally, I cannot think of a greater evil than to sell your children into bondage before they are even conceived.

These paper games are backed by the present and future labor of the American people or, in other words, taxes. The American people are truly paying interest on imaginary wealth. Worse, not a single penny has ever been paid on the principal so the principal continuously increases and interest on the "loans" increases exponentially. The member banks thru the Fed basically control the United States economy and thru the International Monetary Fund, the world.

It is a fixed game, the well connected always win. If they make mistakes, they will receive a government bailout and the taxpayer ultimately pays. It is not just banks that get bailouts but also poorly run corporations, unions and even municipalities. The government used to set the rules of the financial game. Unfortunately, it now actually works the other way around and it is the banks that do. It is the most incredible scam in the history of the world. One has to wonder, since "The Fed" has been such a bad deal for the American people, why doesn't the United States go back to having the Treasury print money directly without the interest payments to private companies? That is a very good question, indeed.

Finance

Be you in what line of life you may, it will be amongst
your misfortunes if you have not time properly to
attend to pecuniary [monetary] matters. Want of attention to these matters has impeded the progress of
science and of genius itself.

~WILLIAM COBBETT

IF WE ARE to embark on the most important endeavor of humanity, we must give some thought as to how it is to be funded. The modern world is hobbled by massive debt, credit cards, mortgages and
loans for everything. It is advertised and promoted and at the behest
of the financial community and even governments are part of the
game. We must consider the alternatives carefully and weigh them
to see how they will fare in the future.

Saving for the future has been replaced by borrowing money, not
from family as has been done in the past but from large banking institutions or government. The lender has control of the hard assets,
such as a house or a car, while the borrower has only a liability and a
monthly payment. The statistics for American households that carry
this debt is over fifteen thousand in credit cards, over one hundred

and fifty thousand for home mortgages and over thirty thousand in student loans. The average American is about eighty thousand dollars in debt and that number does not include public liabilities of over a half million dollars per family in 2013. How can this paradigm be changed to uplift all humanity?

In the last few decades, the Unites States government has been promoting home ownership... "Home ownership is the American dream". In reality, it is a nightmare with a large percentage of the population deeply in debt. A standard thirty-year home mortgage of five and a quarter percent will give the bank a hundred percent profit and you will pay double the purchase price. At nine and a quarter percent you will pay triple and at thirteen percent, common in the 1980's, four times the purchase price. Quite a scam when it is considered that the bank had only imaginary money to lend in the first place.

At the urging of the United States government, banks were giving home mortgages to completely unqualified people. They were being guaranteed by the "Government Sponsored Enterprises" or GSE's. They include Freddy Mac, Fanny Mae for home and commercial property loans and Sallie Mae for huge educational loans. These agencies are little more than arms of the Democratic political party, where party hacks are given huge salaries and bonuses. Control of these vast sums of money gives the party a great deal of political control. These mortgages were then combined into large blocks with "good" and "bad" mortgages and sold as investments to hedge funds then sold to pension funds, cities, States and even foreign governments.

These blocks of what, "shockingly", turned out to be mostly bad mortgages were used to make derivatives. Again, they are wagers as to whether they would increase or decrease in value. All this is a giant paper game, a tower of financial cards that collapses on a regular basis, the latest being in 2008. It was not the first time; there have been banking crisis and calamities thruout history. In the past, troubled banks would simply be taken over by other banks or go out of business, now they are bailed out, repeatedly, by taxpayers.

These problems could be ameliorated if there were far less financial leverage allowed in the system. It is this leverage or the creation of imaginary money and paper assets that allow such things as hostile takeovers and monopolization of industries. This leads to a small number of very large corporations that have control over wide swaths of the world economies. It is what has happened in the banking industry. In the United States, five companies have almost complete control of the economy. It is the same with every industry but even they are owned and controlled by the few large financial companies.

Considering all the turmoil that the current banking system has unleashed upon the world it would seem to be a good idea to consider alternatives. What is needed is an honest banking system not esoteric paper games designed to extract as much as possible from clients. Banks should work as they once did, by lending out their depositors money. They collected interest that was portioned out as a reward to the depositors as well as providing operating expenses and profit for the bank. There are even better alternatives that assume that the borrower and the lender must be equals in risk.

In modern times, banks in Islamic areas have treated their customers better. In all Abrahamic religions, including Judaism, Christianity and Islam there are restrictions in all on borrowing, gambling and getting deeply into debt. They are being ignored by secular bankers more interested in profit. Islamic or Sharia rules may provide a preferable system that would go a long way to prevent paper games that are so common in American and European economies. Laws banning gambling and permanent debt would greatly improve the current banking system. Instead of buying and selling debt, Islamic banking instead provides for risk sharing.

Banking according to Sharia law is the way banking used to be done in Western countries. The banking institution lends out capital and makes a profit on the return while not cheating customers with compounding interest and forcing them to carry all the risk while providing the collateral. Fractional banking is forbidden in Sharia law, as it should be for Jews and Christians, because it is trading something without value. It is fraud; like lending a cow when there is no cow. Only available deposits can be lent out.

The primary concept in Sharia banking is to share and minimize the risk while being fair to the lender and borrower, especially, if their goals are to improve their life and community. Usury or the practice of making unethical loans is forbidden and taking advantage of others misfortunes is considered not only illegal but also immoral. It is the responsibility of the borrower to return what is not theirs; if that is not done it is simply theft.

One of the ways that Sharia banking works is that the bank will purchase the desired item from the seller then allow the buyer to make payments to purchase it from the bank. There are no late penalties so the bank will ask for collateral. The bank may purchase the collateral from the borrower with the understanding to it sell it back at an agreed upon date. There are also leasing and lease-purchase arrangements. This type of banking requires that the borrower not bear all the risk but to share it with the lender. If money is made available to companies, the banks acquire part of the company and payments are made to the bank to purchase it back based upon the profitability of the company. Venture capital can be used to fund an entrepreneur who will provide the ideas and labor while the bank provides the money so that both profit and risk are shared. It is a more balanced distribution of income and does not allow the bankers to monopolize the economy. There are no outrageous bonuses to bank management for taking advantage of clients or taxpayers with bailouts.

An article by Bloomberg writer Lorenzo Totaro reported that the Vatican suggested, "The principles of Islamic finance may represent a possible cure for ailing markets." In other words, it would require a more ethical market that is not trillions and quadrillions in debt. Even tho, it is not Sharia, Iceland has forbidden these practices and put many of their unscrupulous bankers in jail. Fundamentalist Islamic countries such as Iran behead them while the American and European economies continue to be devastated by government policy not to prosecute criminal bankers. The actions of Iceland and Iran tend to make more banking more honest as well as stabilizing their currency. There are Sharia compliant banks, some large and international, that can be found on the Internet.

Instead of the rare gold and silver as a commodity basis for currency, it would make sense to have it based upon something that would directly drive the economy. One item that expands as needed and has real value is the kilowatt-hour, energy is constantly being used. A kilowatt-hour is a measurement of electrical power that can be used to measure any form of energy. The currency would still be called dollars but could be exchanged for energy. If one dollar equals ten kilowatt-hours then a gallon of gasoline or a loaf of good bread would be thirty kilowatt-hours or three dollars. In 2013, one thousand kilowatt-hours is about one hundred dollars. It costs about twelve hundred dollars to produce an ounce of gold or a bit over one megawatt-hour.

The price of a kilowatt-hour varies somewhat with location but this would be dealt with by market forces and a base or standard price and a local premium. This kilowatt-hour over here can be traded or exchanged for a kilowatt-hour over there. They can be exchanged for a labor, a microwave oven or bags of groceries. It could all be tracked thru computerized accounts, which is how banking is done now anyway. It could possibly give the energy companies inordinate power over the economy but they could not possibly be as disastrous as the banking monopolies have been. It would also show who has wealth without the pretense of fiat money.

Currency does not need to have intrinsic value if there is trust between buyers and sellers. Perhaps, that is why the word trust is found in banking so much when there is actually so little of it. It can be enforced by a bond of trust between the government and the citizens, by law or by force or even the laws of nature and probability. It need only be an exchange format, a holder of value between transactions. Nevertheless, the potential for greed and the corruption of those in government is so great other alternatives need to be considered.

An independent, self-reproducing monetary method of exchange that would transcend borders and allow transactions around the world between individuals and organizations would be desirable. It would be used to make purchases and be convertible to currencies or precious metals. It could do this without involving banks or governments. Well, surprise! It exists; and is called a bitcoin or BTC. It was invented in 2009 by a group with the pseudonym Satoshi Nakamoto. It has been said that bitcoins are to central banks as email is to the post office. It is a peer-to-peer network system where transactions are handled electronically thru a "wallet" file or a website. It is a digital currency that can be traded by any two people any where in the world. Because there is no intermediary financial institution, it cannot be manipulated by the unscrupulous.

Bitcoins are based on encryption, not on commodities like silver and gold or debt and bluster like present day national currencies. It is designed to mimic the best of precious metals and currency. It is a medium of exchange solely based upon the acceptance of the participants. The system works with public and private key pairs and cryptographic signatures. When bitcoins are spent by a person or entity a cryptographically signed transaction is created that says "move my bitcoin to this recipient." The public and private keys are transferred with a transaction that then must be verified. When verified, the recipient with the public key can then own that bitcoin.

There can be no cheating and they are extremely difficult to counterfeit because of the cryptographic arrangements of transactions. Each calculation needed to crack a key to a code needs a certain amount of energy. A bitcoin would require, to flip thru the possibilities of the key, a cumulative amount of energy that is a percentage of the entire world's energy production. To attempt to discover the private key would require many times this prodigious amount. They can be stolen if the public key is known. Since they are like cash, the public key must be kept secure by the owner, but instead of a banknote, it is just a number.

The advantages of bitcoins are that they are secure, based upon cryptography with each bitcoin having public and private keys and transactions that are password protected. They are fungible in that every bitcoin is identical to every other bitcoin. They are much more divisible than existing currency; being divided into one hundred million smaller units called satoshi. They are limited with new bitcoins being created on a fixed schedule until the year 2140 when no more can be created.

Anyone can "mine" for new bitcoins by a computationally powerful server that rewards the "miner" with bitcoins for verifying transactions. Transactions must be verified six times before they are valid. In the electronic cyber world, this can happen very quickly. Transactions can be conducted the same as cash anywhere in the world and using the same bitcoin twice is impossible. Once the transaction is completed there is no reversal, it can only be refunded by the recipient.

There are some potential problems that can be foreseen with bitcoins. The biggest is that banks and governments running their scams will consider it a threat. They will, at least, create negative propaganda and take legal action. After all, they control the governments that make the rules of the game. They are ruthless, if they do not get their way; impoverishment, character assassination and murder are all on the table. It has happened many times in history, and I will leave it to you do your own research.

Another problem is that if a system can be cheated someone will figure out how to do it. Hackers seem to enter even into military and corporate computer systems with amazing regularity. It is not uncommon to hear about it on the news. Little harm is done and the weakness that is found is corrected. One can be sure that if anything important were compromised it would not be on the evening news. Actually, it is not as easy as one would expect watching the movies. The bitcoin system was designed by cryptographic engineers and appears to be quite secure and has been tested many times with no lapse in security. Bitcoins have been stolen from inattentive owners and the servers have been shut down by denial of service hacks but the system remained secure and anonymous.

It is possible to have a financial system that is more interested in actually producing something instead of making paper games and stealing from the lower classes. To keep it that way, would require honesty, perseverance and vigilance, the very things that seem to be sorely lacking these days. People need to let their leaders know that they want a safe method of exchange that maintains its value over time.

The colonization of the Moon cannot happen without a way to pay for the materials, fuels and labor. Few projects, even as grand as moving humanity to another world, could be done altruistically. It must be considered how to fund the greatest advance of humanity since the smelting of metal. This goal can easily cost as much as the paper games but with a much grander goal and with far greater and real profits. The money to be made while actually doing something for humanity is astonishing. The profit from the energy production systems that would be developed building cities on the Moon and in Earth and Lunar orbit would be immense. In addition, if it is expensive but desirable we humans will find a better way, we always do.

Tyranny

Government is not reason; it is not eloquent; it is force. Like fire, it is a dangerous servant and a fearful master. Never for a moment should it be left for irresponsible action.

~George Washington

ALL TYPES OF government are in reality, oligarchies; they hide behind the leader and are usually quite secretive. The presumptive leader; call them king, dictator, president or prime minister is in reality just the face of the elites and the oligarchy. They let him take all the accolades for little advances and all the blame when things turn bad. Laws and rules made by the oligarchy are generally for the benefit of the elites with little regard given to the citizenry. The leader may change but the oligarchy never does. Government is commonly a vehicle for the elites and their oligarchy to enrich themselves and control the citizenry. In many places such as Europe and Southeast Asia, there are layers and layers of government centuries deep.

There are deliberate misconceptions in modern politics, promoted in the media and the government itself. The terms Left wing and Right wing are a fine example. They date to late Eighteenth Century French revolutionary era. The President of the National Assembly, looking to his right were supporters of the king and historical stability and to his left were supporters of the revolution and undefined change. These terms have been misused and along with liberal and conservative are now just labels in modern politics. Those with an agenda to confuse an already apathetic electorate use these and other words. One of the many tools used to manipulate the citizenry.

The actual endpoints of political thought are no government and all government, anarchy to totalitarianism. The spectrum is from each citizen controlling their own destiny to the government controlling the destiny of citizens. Anarchy and totalitarianism are not ideal situations to advance technology and society. In either case, individuals cannot take advantage and nurture their own ideas.

The majority of governments in the world today are totalitarian and repressive. They are repressive in that there are more controls on the actions of citizens than on the actions of government. The repressive government can be monarchist, fascist or democratic; the result is all the same. There is little difference between serving a king, dictator, president or prime minister. They all represent the state and can make the same rules and laws that essentially have the same result. They can also be benign and exert little control but that is generally temporary. If there are no restrictions, government power and size will continue to expand.

There are shades of gray between the endpoints that would allow the most personal growth for individual and groups of citizens. The government can provide stability without being authoritarian. Unfortunately, small libertarian governments tend not to be stable over time. It is because of the lust for money and power of some. It can only last if there are strict limits or rewards, either legal or cultural that would prevent the growth of governmental size and power.

Corruption and the growth of government is a major problem in most countries in the world. Some have laws to keep it under control but those laws, such as the Constitution of the United States, are constantly under pressure. The Finance Minister of Nigeria, Ngozi Okonjo-Iweala, said in an interview, "... Some of the things that are looked upon as corruption over there [Nigeria] have found legal and professional names over here, in the United States. For instance, at home when people go to lawmakers and induce them with trips and gifts and so on to pass legislation, it is called corruption. But in the U.S. it's actually a profession called lobbying!"

She is not the only one that notices the goings-on. Pundits find humor in it and call the various bars and restaurants where the politicians and lobbyists meet in Washington, DC the K-Street Whorehouse. Governments... all governments, are inherently and fundamentally incompetent and corrupt. Even compromise is corrupt, "I'll help you get what you want if you help me get what I want." Any feigned interest in citizens well being can be attributed to their interest in power and more importantly, money.

So-called progressives in the early twentieth century, indeed to this day, are little more than fascists with eugenic tendencies. The history of the Twentieth Century shows that progressivism always leads inexorably to human rights abuses and tyranny. Sadly, they are still with us, all the might and money of the United States is manipulated by a mere 269 easily corruptible people. They have "reinterpreted" the US Constitution that previously explicitly limited the power of central authority.

There is a never-ending cycle of growth, projects and programs are started with lots of money made available by groups of politicians that benefit from them, their cronies and occasionally their constituencies. New groups of politicians come along with new projects and programs that sometimes take money and influence from the old. The old are never shut down, even if they are shown to be detrimental and even destructive, because if they were it would mean that it was an artifice in the first place.

New programs are added to the old programs and over the years it gets pretty darn expensive to maintain all this waste. There are many fine examples in the United States of programs started by politicians such as Social Security, "War on Poverty", "War on Drugs", ethanol subsidies, medical programs, housing loans, school loans, farm loans as well as many "disability" programs. These programs are generally little more than scams or power grabs. There are "green" companies started with the help of "government" money. Almost all of these taxpayer supported companies go bankrupt with huge bonuses for the management and huge losses to the taxpayer.

There are several types of repressive governments, some more obvious than others. There are countries to this day where the monarch maintains absolute power and the monarch is the same as the "state". Examples of this are Saudi Arabia, Kuwait, Oman, Qatar, Swaziland and Brunei. Most dictatorships are hereditary with leadership positions held by family members and as such are little different from monarchies. Dictator is rarely an official title, "president", "chancellor" or even "general" are preferred, presumably, for the pretense and propaganda. There are quite a number of these at the moment; some of the worse are North Korea, Syria, Cuba, Sudan, Zimbabwe, Chad, Burma and Turkmenistan.

Democracy is another form of repressive government where the "majority" makes rules and laws for the "minority". In fact, in a democracy fifty-one percent of the population can enslave the other forty-nine percent. One must keep in mind that slavery flourished under the "democratic" United States for its first seventy years then segregation for almost another century. There is so much governmental propaganda and voter fraud there are few actual democracies. It is not "power to the people" where the people are sovereign, but power to those that have the best party line and political machine to sway the majority.

Modern "democratic" governments operate on the principals of patronage and intimidation. Politicians hide behind the sobriquet of a "democratic" government and once elected they surprisingly become tools of the ruling class. Democracy is, perhaps the greatest tyranny of them all. A quote, sometimes attributed to Benjamin Franklin, is "Democracy is not freedom. Democracy is two wolves and a lamb voting on what to have for lunch."

In the United States the Democratic Party uses the tool of democracy to pander to groups of "minorities" who have real or imagined past grievances. It includes groups like African Americans who have actually suffered under (Democratic Party) racism. They have even created "minorities" out of such groups as Mexicans and Central Americans who are simply in the country illegally. They receive benefits that most citizens do not get to motivate them to vote "correctly", i.e. for the Democrat party. The list includes taxpayer funded housing, food, medical care and discretionary spending money. Superficially, it would seem that the government is protecting these citizens and non-citizens from the consequences of their own foibles but they are kept in conditions of no security and poor education in what are, in reality, breeding barracks where they turn out the next generation of dependence and "voters".

Young women dependent on government programs are financially encouraged to have more children and young men have no responsibility beyond supplying sperm. In the United States they fill prisons to the point that there are now more Americans incarcerated, per capita, than Soviet Russia at the height of the Stalinist terror. The reality is that they are being bought off and contained with the illusion of being middle class without putting forth any effort for their "votes". Moreover, in many cases, their votes are fraudulently written in by the political party in control. It is even called a political machine to keep the gangsters in power. The city of Chicago is a fine example.

The modern political tool of government largess evolved from socialism and collectivism. It has expanded from its beginnings in radical unionism in Europe in the mid Nineteenth Century, presumably, to solve the evils caused by rapid industrialization. The political machines stepped in and took over the ultimate responsibility of the care and feeding of "needy" citizens, something that families, churches and other organizations had done in the past. The siren's song of socialism solving the ills of mankind is not just ineffective; it has the opposite effect creating dependence and indolence.

The only places that arguably have had even a bit of success with socialism are countries like those in Scandinavia. They have small wealthy homogeneous populations and a reasonably honest government. Even there it is being overused by some natives and by a large number of immigrants. The concept of a "safety net" to catch those in need gives justification to increase the size and power of government. Swedish taxes are sixty percent or more but they are explicit, everyone knows about them. In other counties, they are almost as high but they are hidden as "user fees" and other taxes or, worse, governmental borrowing which is a tax on future generations.

One of the many problems created by socialism is called the free rider problem. The name comes from the unfairness of public transportation where paying passengers have to pay for themselves plus the free riders. The problem is that some use government services and do not pay for them. The effect grows as more and more people take advantage of any "free" services provided. As the number of people getting services grows and grows other problems come to fore, including who is going to pay for all the largesse. It may come as a surprise but there is nothing free from the government... nothing. The money always has to come from somewhere and it is always from productive citizens, or worse, "borrowed" (stolen) from future generations.

Socialism is not stable because ever more people getting "free" government services, allowed to vote, will demand more government services. The money and dwindling resources will need to be allocated to the more "connected" groups. Others are left out and become agitated and totalitarianism must ensue to control the population. As resources become scarce, revolution or war will be the usual outcome.

Propaganda from the more or less government controlled media and education tells us that fascism, such as in Germany, Italy and Spain of the early mid-Twentieth Century was "rightist" and therefore different from collectivism on the "left". Fascism and its offshoot Nazism, as they were applied are certainly forms of collectivism, altho socialists and self-styled "progressives" decry the association.

Benito Mussolini was a member of the Italian Socialist Party and had the concept of fascism reinvented from the Roman Empire. It was to give him the power to implement socialism on a national scale. As the single leader, he wanted to be able to "strike against the backwardness of the right and the destructiveness of the left". The horrible civil war in Spain was a conflict between Franco's fascist socialists and a strange alliance of republicans, communists and anarchists. A case can be made that World War 2 and the associated conflicts were actually wars between factions of big government socialists.

Adolf Hitler's political party copied fascist theories from the Italian dictator Mussolini and called itself the National Socialist Worker's Party. The nickname, Nazi, in English, is from the German pronunciation. The Nazi party was able to take control of the German government in 1933 by pandering to the unions and capitalists at the same time (sound familiar?). Hitler did not forbid unions as some would like you think. He combined them into larger entities controlled by his government. This rhetoric was later downplayed and German capitalists became willing cronies when wartime spending increased their profit margins.

The Nazis were not only eugenicists following the American example of Alexander Graham Bell, Stanford president David Starr Jordan and Margaret Sanger and their ilk but also some of the first environmentalists. Their ideology is still around; the present day Green party is an offshoot of the Nazi party. It is interesting that fascism would be the only embarrassment for collectivists. The communist Russians,

Chinese and Cambodians caused many more deaths, albeit from murder and starvation of their own people rather than war. In countries around the world experimentation with collectivism have been murderous failures.

A good case can be made that Franklin Roosevelt's America was another socialist fascist state. Using the excuse of war, the government took control of industry and agriculture. In fact, in 1942, there were more people in Roosevelt's prison camps than Hitler's concentration camps. It was not just a large number of Japanese Americans but also Germans, Italians and, historically, indigenous Americans. At the behest of the United States government, these groups were also removed from Latin American countries. Some were put into interment camps in the United States where they were subjected to forced labor. Many more had their property seized and were expelled to find their own way to a safe location. Even now, the United States has more people imprisoned per capita than any other country on Earth. More people than the Soviet Union during the Stalinist purges.

The United States spends more money on military than most of rest of the world combined, an absolutely astonishing amount of money. The question is; why is all that firepower needed and who is it protecting? The answer is the ruling oligarchy, who profit mightily from what United States President Eisenhower called the "Military Industrial Complex". To the average citizen it doesn't matter who is at the top; the effects on them are all the same. If you are one of the oligarchs, living in any country can be pleasant compared to the general population.

Government involvement is required in most transactions including purchases and agreements and contracts. The reason is that governments make laws that are meant to be broken. The government can't tyrannize innocent people. Since the only power government has is force and to legitimize that force there must be laws broken. When there isn't enough crime and criminals, more laws will be made.

There will be so many laws that it becomes impossible to go thru life without breaking some of them. The government doesn't want a nation of law-abiding citizens; it wants control and power.

The elites don't stand idle, they compete with one another for even more wealth and power but they also take the conflict to the citizens and they are the ones that suffer. The Twentieth Century was the bloodiest periods of human history. There were conflicts between repressive socialist governments, oppression of their own citizens and genocide. One needs to keep in mind that governments were then as now, controlled by elites. Revolutions and civil wars were common, many establishing fascist, socialist, democratic, and communist forms of government. The death toll of these conflicts, strife and famine was well over two hundred million.

The worst problem of modern governments is that they have horrendous spending and borrowing problems to support all the activities that they should not be doing in the first place. These activities include such things as creating government dependence, embezzling, nepotism and supporting cronies in the guise of providing services. The fastest growing segment of governmental expenditure is interest on debt that requires even more debt to maintain itself, an unsustainable situation. All this money and interest is being paid by future generations, we are truly bathing in the sweat and blood of our own children.

There is an old adage that taxes are a fine for doing good and fines are a tax for doing bad. Taxes and fines are used to direct citizenry into activities that are preferred by those that make money from the government. Some taxation or governmental revenue generation is necessary but it should only be enough to operate essential governmental activities. The power of government can be overwhelming and unrelenting and there must be laws that cannot be circumvented to limit its power.

Governance

"...whenever the people are well-informed, they can
be trusted with their own government; that, when-
ever things get so far wrong as to attract their notice,
they may be relied on to set them right."

~THOMAS JEFFERSON

ALL THE LACK of ethics, evil and mayhem aside, governments have done good things from time to time, improving the lives of their citizens. They are usually done in response to some sort of crisis. The London sewer and sanitary systems were built because of several cholera outbreaks; most every modern city and town has them now. Subways were built because of inadequate transportation. The first was, again, in London in 1863 when walking and horse drawn carriages were still the dominant transportation. Intercontinental railways were built to grab and hold land, move freight and armies. The Moon landings in the 1960's were the result of a military — industrial race between the United States and the Soviet Union. The Internet was invented by a division of the United States Department of Defense as a way for Universities and defense contractors to communicate.

On the other hand, why are there popular revolutions and what are the people looking for? In almost every case, it is freedom, but from what? Freedom is a catchphrase for propagandists but how many people understand what it means? It is freedom from government! It is to be free from an authority that mandates people do as they are told, to be a certain religion or to behave in an obligatory way. It is freedom, above all, from a rapacious oligarchy that clings to power by any means. It is freedom from the excesses of government. It is citizens being allowed to own their own property, raise their children, take risks and start businesses without excessive regulation and taxation. Freedom comes from the recognition of certain rights that may not be taken away, not even by a majority vote. Over the centuries, people have yearned for freedom from the rapaciousness of the oligarchs; wars and revolutions have been fought over it.

The primary goal of government should be to govern, that is providing guidance and organization. Its proper role should be to provide a framework of security to mediate conflicts and prevent citizens and organizations from being molested by other citizens or organizations. It should prevent growth and overreach of the government that leads directly to corruption. Governments should not be involved in charity, "safety nets", healthcare, and social security all of which lead to huge "slush funds" and destructive behavior. All of these things can be done by family and actual charities at the local level, which provide aid when needed and guidance toward more productive activities. In short, governments need to be able maintain fairness, honesty and remain small so they will last the test of time.

There is a permissive libertarian capitalist form of governing called minarchism also known as minimal statism or even a night-watchman state. It is there to be sure that things do not get out of hand. Minarchists maintain that the government is necessary but that its only legitimate function is the protection of individuals from aggression, theft, fraud and breach of contract. The government has no authority to use its monopoly of force to interfere with reasonable transactions.

The legal profession, in many ways, is overrepresented in government. One of the ways the legal system works is that it sets up or defines a conflict with a protagonist and an antagonist. Law firms have a money making device called billable hours; any excuse is used to add to a client's bill making legal costs more expensive. This is especially true in business and corporate law where disputes can be carried on for years. The problem is that there are too many lawyers in the United States who are all trying to make a prosperous living. This is carried over into government service creating ethics problems because they foment disputes where none existed.

A person should be free to do as they choose without harming others. Citizens should be free to assure their own survival as well as the survival of their family and group. It espouses small local government with far less government control. A minarchist government is, necessarily, a libertarian government. If an individual wants to destroy themselves with drugs and other high-risk behaviors, there are no rules other than the restraints of family, friends and community. In an educated population, this activity should be rare.

Minarchism in its most basic form has, as the only government officials, a system of courts and police to carry out the orders of the courts. The will of the many cannot be imposed on individuals that do not impinge on others. Services such as fire departments and prisons could be included but these services can also be provided by profit and non-profit organizations. A laissez faire approach to the economy would lead to prosperity for all those that wish to work toward their goals. It would allow people and organizations to succeed or fail if they don't perform. There are no big government safety nets to catch you when you fail. One takes responsibility or depends upon relatives, friends and community who will help correct problems.

There are minimal laws in a minarchist system, a bill of rights would be sufficient so that everyone knows their limits so as to not affect others without their permission. Community customs and judicial precedence would count for a great deal. Judgeships would be an elected position. Complaints against one citizen or organization against another would be taken to a judge or a tribunal for consideration as to which party has been injured. There would be appeals to tribunals of an odd number of judges or there could be juries of informed and involved citizens.

The court system would be supported by a loser pays legal costs arrangement that would include the court ordered actions by the judges. The costs involved would also limit the number of appeals. Rich and poor alike would receive equal treatment with the proviso that judges can be kept honest and free from intimidation. If it could be made so it is in the best interests of the rich to keep the courts honest, then they will be. If there were communities of intelligent, involved and ethical people a minarchist system would work with little modification. Regrettably, in the real world at this point in history this type of person in politics is a rarity.

There is a minarchist system of sorts in operation all over the world. It is a condominium association where a purchase contract is signed to obey the bylaws. Each owner gets one vote for the board of directors who then elects the president. The members of the association are free to do as they wish within their property but the common areas are subject to the rules of the association because they are supported by association dues. They generally work well over time but there are various legal actions available to the association and the members if disputes can't be resolved. It is much like a minarchist government, the president of the association is the judge who makes most of the decisions, but can be overridden by the board of directors. There can be competing factions but that is not necessarily a bad thing. The problem with this form of government is that on a larger scale, considering human nature, it could quickly become nepotistic, corrupted or worse. It would become more concerned with maintaining itself than serving the citizens. There is also the problem of the residents becoming lazy and a management company is contracted. It works out well for disengaged people but it does cost more than self-management.

Perhaps, a minarchist government would be workable for local governments within a larger framework that would allow governments to check each other to prevent the growth of corruption. Again, this type of government does not help or hurt anyone that is not bothering anyone else. It is a government in the purest sense of the word in that it is a source of organization and management not a service provider or charity. Minarchist judges could be selected by various means including replacement based upon merit.

A meritocracy is a form of administrative leadership where individual advancement is based upon abilities. These merits, such as, intelligence, education, motivation, experience and even physical ability would be determined with evaluations and examinations. It simply accepts the way society actually works with the brightest and most vigorous people, if allowed, rising to positions of leadership. It is not a new concept but similar to philosophy of Confucius, the earliest meritocracy was the Han dynasty in China about 200 BC. The modern version was refined in the Twentieth Century by British socialist and politician Michael Young. He considered the possibility of a United Kingdom where positions of leadership were filled by merit and not social strata.

A more expansive form of government would include a legislature and an executive as well as courts (sound familiar?). There could also be a set of minimum rules or guidelines that all would be required to obey, that is, a constitution. In this fashion a minarchist government evolves into a constitutional republic. A republic is a form of government where affairs of the government are public and not the privileged concern of government officials. There are no secrets and the citizenry can make themselves aware of the inner workings. A republic is set up to protect individual rights over the mob or elites. Unfortunately, a government that calls itself a republic may not actually be one.

Governments should be associated with human rights that are not only slogans; they need to be written in a document such as a "Bill of Rights". The United States was founded as a constitutional republic, that is, the individual chooses his wants and desires within a framework of laws that protects the individual citizen as well as citizens from one another. A constitution is the foundation of laws to secure the status and rights of every individual. If the constitution and the rule of law are not vigorously defended, the constitutional republic devolves into democracy and totalitarianism, as has certainly happened in the United States.

The US Constitution may have been on the right track with guaranteed human rights but the democracy part of it allowed such things as slavery, segregation, government dependence and overspending. If the constitution were followed, as written, there would have been no slavery. It was a document written explicitly to put limits on the power of the government but in the end, greed has won. The best concept put forth in the Constitution is that we are all created equal, and as such, are equal under law and there should be no special citizens. The government, in general, should not be taking from one group of citizens and giving it to others.

Another form of government is a corporation where people own shares and vote according to the number of shares. It has the effect of making it well known who the elites or majority shareholders are. Shareholders have the power to elect a board of directors. The shareholders and the board choose administrative officials such as the chief executive officer or CEO. This type of government can as a dictatorship with the board and the shareholders making the more important decisions such as replacing the CEO, if necessary. Dictatorships are not always bad especially if the leader is an enlightened despot and keeps a reign on corruption. Rules could be written into the corporate charter to prevent it from becoming totalitarian and everyone maintains their rights. An advantage or disadvantage is that if you don't own a share you don't participate. Corporations have internal mechanisms to minimize corruption and embezzlement because it increases expenses and lowers profits.

It would be in our interest to conjecture what form of government would be the best for our extraterrestrial communities. Some form of a semi-democratic constitutional meritocracy would combine some good ideas. It is understood that many people are lazy and let others do their job for them, which includes watching over the government. As Thomas Jefferson said "History, in general, only informs us what bad government is".

Government can be a positive force. One of the biggest problems to be solved; is how to redirect elites and their tools in government away from self-aggrandizing goals. Move them to positive goals such as uplifting of all people with education and meaningful employment. People can have dignity and work to improve themselves and their community, there is certainly enough to do. These goals can cost as much as wars and with huge amounts of real wealth to be made for everyone. Perhaps, the elites could rethink their and roles and contemplate the goal of moving humanity off the planet.

A secondary goal is that governments need to be able to maintain these positive goals for long periods without the growth of corruption. There are no perfect governments; the best ones allow the most freedom for the citizens while protecting them from each other. This goal could be written into a constitution that would also have iron-clad rules to control the growth of government.

There needs to be a system of safeguards to prevent the takeover of the government by the unscrupulous. Small governments with small budgets do not attract gangsters unless they see an opening or an invitation. These safeguards would reduce the power and wealth of the oligarchies so, sadly, it is unlikely to be possible without their

blessing and assistance. When rulers see their self-interest in working for the citizens things can change a great deal. There have been
enlightened leaders that were thinking more about their people and
their nation than themselves. Nelson Mandela, George Washington,
Ho Chi Minh, Charles de Gaulle, Giuseppe Garibaldi, Mustafa Atatürk,
Kwame Nkruma, Mahatma Gandhi and Thomas Jefferson are some
that come to mind.

The elites and their minions in government need not be unrelent-
ingly avaricious. Government can be a tool to unite people and can
gather up huge sums of money and organize great works that benefit
humanity. There are many examples: the Suez and Panama Canals,
the high-speed rail systems around Europe, the manned space missions. Of course, governmental projects tend to be inefficient with
more than a little graft, but they sometimes manage to do the job.
In fact, one can tell a better government by the fact that they do get
some of the things done that they say they will do.

Capitalism can be broken when there are no rules against an
enterprise moving from a community to a lower cost area and it is
give a reason to do so. The control of expenses becomes more important when a large percentage of corporate income is derived from
evading excess taxes. Since everyone that works in the company pays
taxes, it is counterproductive to make the corporation as a whole
pay even more. The enterprise must raise the price of their product
to compete, in effect becoming a tax collector for the government.
Sadly, the other option is to move to a more business friendly area,
which happens all too often.

One needs to consider what forms of government have existed
and what forms have worked out the best for productive and indus-
trious people. That would include how to keep the greed of the elites
under control and what form would be best for humanity to move
onto colonizing the Moon and expanding into the Universe? Because
of its utmost importance, the preeminent organization is one whose
goal is to move humanity off the planet. The government can help

but it should be with the most amount of personal liberty and the least amount of death and destruction.

Perhaps, it is wishful thinking to believe that it is possible to change the direction of existing governments. It may be possible that they could be convinced to support the return to the days of space travel if it is seen it be in their best interests to redirect the efforts of humanity to a greater goal. In any case, it would seem that any type of government will work but the best results will come from those that are ethical.

Evolution

"Today the human race is a single twig on the tree of life, a single species on a single planet. Our condition can thus only be described as extremely fragile, endangered by forces of nature currently beyond our control, our own mistakes, and other branches of the wildly blossoming tree itself. Looked at this way, we can then pose the question of the future of humanity on Earth, in the solar system, and in the galaxy from the standpoint of both evolutionary biology and human nature. The conclusion is straightforward: Our choice is to grow, branch, spread and develop, or stagnate and die."

~ROBERT ZUBRIN, ENTERING SPACE, 1999

ORGANISMS CHANGE OR mutate over time. The most mutation occurs when there is a change in the environment because the rate of mortality increases. Any change in an organism will not continue if the organism does not reproduce. If it does, the change could go on to the next generation and so on. Death and reproduction drive evolution. Evolution is actually a misnomer; it does not advance an organism to some unknown perfection. It produces what works to survive in its environment. All that needs to happen is for it to survive long enough to continue its genetic legacy. There are creatures that appeared on Earth hundreds of millions years ago that are still all around us.

It is the same with humans; our large brains aside, we are not genetically more advanced than other organisms. Our ancestors survived long enough to breed and ensure the survival of the young. Organisms have special abilities that help them adapt to their environments and humans are, again, no different. We have some specialties that other creatures do not have.

Human evolution has been happening quickly. Humans have about five times the number of mutations that would be expected of a creature our size. As stated by Bruce Lahn at the university of Chicago "To accomplish so much in so little evolutionary time - a few tens of millions of years - requires a selective process that is perhaps categorically different from the typical processes of acquiring new biological traits."

Human evolution is now continuing, to borrow computer terms, not only in the usual way in "wetware" or biology but also in "hardware" or machinery and "software", knowledge. It is continuing most rapidly technologically and there is a necessity to do so for the usual reason, a changing environment. More humans than ever are living in urban environments; many are not required to fend for themselves in any way. In science fiction, rapidly becoming fact, three general types of humans are conjectured. The first are the wild humans or the unmodified, allowing natural evolution to continue. The second are people who whose bodies are augmented by mechanisms and third are those augmented by biology.

Wild humans, perhaps for religious reasons, would choose to remain unmodified following the original evolutionary form. Perhaps, economics would prevent them from taking advantage of advances in science and medicine. Even in the "wild" state humans will slowly continue to mutate and evolution will favor those who survive and reproduce the most. Mutations and the evolution of humanity continue but biological change is much too slow to be noticeable in a few generations. However, we are beginning to evolve ourselves. Evolution is continuing with our newfound knowledge and understanding of genetics, biological systems and microminiaturized electronics.

There are people who rely upon electronics and machinery to expand their human abilities, called Mechanists by Bruce Sterling in his book "Schismatrix". It seems quite plausible because it is already happening. They would have devices attached to their bodies like the "Borgs" or cybernetic humans of Star Trek fame. These devices become like part of the body because humans have the ability to empathize with machinery. Studies have shown that after a period of adaptation amputees with artificial limbs soon accept the prosthesis as one of their own body parts.

There have been operational prosthetics such as glasses, arms, legs and teeth for centuries. More recent development include, hearing amplifiers, speech synthesizers, motorized chairs and mechanized arms and legs. There has been a great deal of research into electrical connections to nerves; man-machine interfaces. We have electronics that are attached to us even now, such as wrist watches, the most advanced form are smart phones. They certainly aid in information gathering and communications. Photographs and videos are far more reliable and detailed reminders of events than human memory.

It appears that it is possible to connect devices and have them directly controlled by the brain. It appears that the perception will be that it will feel "natural" like any other appendage. Machines both simple and complex have been aiding human muscle power ever since Homo sapiens evolved. We project ourselves into our machines and they seem to become part of us as in wielding a machete or riding a bicycle.

There are technologies that help the disabled and even help keep people alive. There are perhaps a million people with artificial heart valves and another three million worldwide living with heart pacemakers. There are almost a thousand people living with artificial hearts; there would be more but they are quite expensive. Other artificial organs are in development.

There are machines that allow humans to "see" outside of the usual visual spectrum. Night vision goggles amplify the available light so that it is possible to see by starlight. There are heat vision as well as ultraviolet and other high-energy sensors. These devices translate the previously useable energies into our visual spectrum. There is the Argus system where there the retina in some blind people can be stimulated by a retinal implant that receives a signal from a camera. There are devices that allow humans to swim with the fish for short amounts of time. Scuba tanks and regulators as well as rebreathers, that chemically remove carbon dioxide, are available and common technologies. This technology has led to spacesuits that allow to wearer to survive in the vacuum of space.

There are implants that can be installed in what is left of the nerves and musculature of amputees to control a prosthetic arm or leg. Some of them are now able to be controlled by a direct implant in the brain. Since an artificial arm or leg can be directly controlled by the brain it would seem that the ability could be extended to any other machine such as a backhoe or a drone aircraft. These trends will continue as these devices become more and more available and cost effective. There is little doubt that we will invent our successors and that they will be some sort of human – machine hybrid. Many of our descendants in the future will be composite beings of living biology and living electronics.

Steven Hawking is a brilliant English physicist, who apparently solves multidimensional mathematical equations in his head and probes the structure of the Universe. Perhaps, he should have died in his forties after being diagnosed with Lou Gehrig's disease. Instead, with the help of drugs and electronics, he communicates, is mobile and has survived well into old age. During his long life he has contributed mightily to human knowledge.

Transplants could be considered similar to electronic implants because they are from other than the person's own body, that is, another person or animal's body. There has been much progress in transgenic and mechanical hearts as well as other various body parts such as hips and knees. Mechanical replacements are not being developed as quickly as was once envisioned and it appears that biology may soon outpace robotics. A Maryland man has been living for more than thirty years with a human heart transplant. . Of course, there are the usual phony ethical considerations. If a loved one was in need of a new heart and the only thing preventing it was a self-styled ethicist, perhaps it should be considered manslaughter.

There has been research into transgenic transplants, particularly from pigs, that have been genetically modified so that they can survive in a human body. They can be used as temporary lifesavers or as permanent replacements. There is a developing technology to create organs from the body's own tissue: biological replacements grown from stem cells. There will be no rejection issues so the patient will not have to take powerful drugs to shut down their immune systems. Of course, there will be no ethical problems because the host is the donor.

There has been a good deal of study of nanomachines, whose working parts are the size of a billionth of a meter or about the size of a protein molecule. To make machinery that small is an ambitious task. To understand the scale, if a grain of salt were magnified to the size of a large warehouse a white blood cell would be the size of an automobile and a red blood cell the size of a tire. An average bacterium would be the size of a hot dog, a virus a pea and a protein molecule a grain of salt.

Nanomachines would provide benefits like the bacterial flora that already inhabits the human body. They would be able to move around the body in the bloodstream and be programmed to accomplish tasks. Presently, nanomachines have no moving parts and are limited to drug delivery but eventually they will be able to manipulate biological materials. They could make permanent residence in the human body to keep harmful organisms under control and make repairs that the human body does not, for example, they will be able to remove plaque from blood vessels.

Sterling also speculated "Shapers" who used eugenics, modified biology and training to become more survivable. Again, this is already happening. There are attributes that can be enhanced by training, drugs and practice such as making better soldiers, musicians, dancers and athletes. Many other human attributes can used to please each other, such as the pleasure and calming of physical therapy, sex and gastronomy.

There are sports that involve superior capabilities including weight lifting, swimming, track and gymnastics. It certainly amazes when one has seen the beauty of motion as gymnasts, snowboarders and, certainly, parkour practitioners who make seemingly impossible jumps as they move over and around obstacles. These and other capabilities are available to all humans but there is always room for improvement as well as something completely new and different.

Shapers could also have heighted intelligence and training in new and different states of mind. They would be "ninja" thespians that can control their voices and body language to communicate with each other on a deeper level. They could also influence the state of mind of untrained humans. This is happening now to a lesser degree and is available for all to see in the production studios and theaters of the world.

Humanity could mutate though biological means, including manipulating ourselves with genetic engineering. The sciences of medicine and genetics have been expanding greatly for the last few decades. What were once miracle cures have become common and people are restored to health from some disfiguring or fatal malady.

Genetics can also be used to enhance existing traits or give new abilities to individuals and their offspring. It can be used to reduce the effects of aging or even reverse it.

Mutations can be installed in the human genome that would give humans special abilities. We can then adapt our bodies to a multitude of environments. Humans can give themselves the ability to prevent bone mass loss in weightless and low gravity environment. Conceivably, we can also give ourselves another set of hands where our feet are. Unlike the other great apes, our feet were evolved for long distance running but the anatomy of a gibbon would be much better adapted to move about in a weightless environment. Perhaps, using gene splicing we can create a race of human – gibbon hybrids. If that is possible, we can install larger lungs or even gills and cold bloodedness so that we can survive and even dwell underwater.

Human hibernation is one of the gifts we can bestow upon ourselves. It would give us the ability to dampen down the fires of life in emergencies. Hibernation in mammals is common in many species to survive times of food scarcity. It has even been discovered in primitive primates, particularly the fat tailed dwarf lemur that hibernates for several months in the dry season. Interestingly, the human body already has a cold-water suspended animation response where temperature, and breathing and the heart slow down and death by drowning can sometimes be averted. It should be used more often in life saving situations to prevent brain damage during strokes and heart attacks. It can also be used for long space flights to minimize the required supplies.

Human senses can be expanded; an example is that we have poor color vision compared to some other creatures, notably birds. Our red and green color receptors are close in hue because they evolved from the same receptor. Humans and some monkeys can see three colors. Most mammals have only two-color vision because they evolved from nocturnal creatures. Many others including aquatic mammals, can only see shades of gray. Many birds and some reptiles have four-color vision and the response of the receptors has more evenly spaced spectrum. It should be possible to give humans the ability to see in four colors. It is now known that a small percentage of women have something approaching this ability. Vision can even be expanded to other parts of the electromagnetic spectrum such as infrared and ultraviolet that some other animals use.

Genes and traits can be transferred between species. Spider silk can't be harvested similarly to moth larvae cocoons used in the silk industry because they are cannibalistic. The University of Wyoming has transferred the ability to make spider dragline silk protein into goats. The goats are milked and the protein is purified. This procedure can be applied to any creature that has Earthly genetics because we all share the same evolution. It is a bit surprising to know that that we humans share half of our genetics with a banana.

Trees and even rabbits have been genetically engineered to make proteins that cause them to glow in the dark. Glowing rabbits may not have much utility but the trees could light our way and even replace streetlights. If rabbits can glow, so can humans, which may be interesting, but not very useful. We have the technology to transfer the ability to produce proteins but not structures such as gills and wings. Biological structures are not associated with just a single gene but a complicated arrangement of genes that need to be turned on or off at an appropriate time of development. There needs to be more study and research but it is certainly not impossible.

It will soon be possible to retrofit living creatures with new genetics that would grow and become part of their body. There is a great deal of confidence that we are very close to having all the technology to change our body shape and chemistry by design. We will be able to modify our senses genetically and intelligence itself. The most important human trait that separates us from other animals, not in kind, but in ability is intelligence. Perhaps, our modified brains may be able to truly understand quantum physics or visualize four or more dimensions of freedom.

Antidote

We humans are an extremely important manifesta-
tion of the replication bomb, because it is through
us - through our brains, our symbolic culture and our
technology - that the explosion may proceed to the
next stage and reverberate through deep space.

~Richard Dawkins

IN ORDER FOR the latest medical miracles to become available
for the majority of people there needs to be solutions to the availability and high cost of health care. Solutions would embrace increasing the general wealth as well as reducing medical expenses. There
must also be a change in attitude. The change in attitude entails the
realization that healthcare is a personal responsibility like personal
hygiene such as bathing and teeth brushing.

Healthcare is not a right but something that has to have effort
expended and even paid for. Plumbing and airconditioning are not
considered civil rights and the services of a medical technician are
not either. The cost of healthcare must be considered as a living
expense. It needs to be budgeted, as are other necessities such as
housing and food. Too often, it is ignored when we are young and

seemingly endlessly healthy. A doctor visit can be less expensive than airconditioning or plumbing repairs but the costs quickly escalate.

The field of medicine has made extraordinary progress but is too expensive for many people to take advantage of it. The cost of a simple stay in a hospital can quickly increase to more than the cost of a new car. The cost of a significant surgical procedure can exceed the cost of a house. The cost of something like a transplant or an artificial heart can balloon to be more than a lifetime income. These costs, in many cases, are incurred with an ambiguous outcome. It may be a big success or it might be a failure and the patient dies or the patient can be an invalid for the remainder of their lives.

The cost of medical procedures has trended upward with advances in technology but also with ever more government involvement and the cost of legal fees. There are concerns with governments becoming involved with healthcare as there is a great potential for corruption and substandard service. If you have waited in a crowded Social Security office, imagine if they had life and death control over you. It is far better to have programs at the community level. It goes back to the strength and resources of the family structure that has been torn apart by socialist governments.

One of the problems is that there are not enough doctors or medical technicians including nurses. In the United States, it costs a great deal of money to be educated to be a physician; it is related to the expense of advanced education overall. It is especially difficult if their income is to be dictated by the government after all of the effort. In other areas of the world, it is much less costly for the medical student. In many countries, people with the aptitude are supported by government programs. The path to becoming a medical doctor is also much quicker. In the U.S. and Canada, it takes eight years or more to become a licensed physician. In places, such as India or Germany it can be five years or less. One of the differences is that the former require an undergraduate degree before even entering medical school. Unquestionably, it is a waste of time, money and talent.

One of the best methods of funding medical degrees is having communities or hospitals provide it thru university programs. The potential doctor or nurse signs a contract to provide service to the funding organization for a period of three to five years after getting their license to practice. It is not only a boon for the organization or community but also provides a clear, secure path for the healthcare professional. The student would also be able to continue their lives while studying without the need for long hours every day. They would also be able to get the needed education more quickly. The reduced cost and time of education would be passed along to patients.

Another problem that increases the cost of healthcare is the cost of drugs and procedures. Companies that invest in research need to be compensated for their efforts and risk. The expense of development needs to be amortized over a period of time, but also, the drug needs to be available to those who need it without the high cost. There are the so-called orphan drugs that are used to treat rare diseases that do not have the sales volume to compensate the pharmaceutical company. The United States and many other countries are giving tax credits, grants and exclusive rights for seven years to cover the cost of development. The cost of drugs is still a heavy burden especially if they need to be taken for the course of ones life.

Solutions need to be found to make necessary drugs available to those that need them. Tax benefits would be helpful for companies that would develop them. Unfortunately, American companies already pay some of the highest corporate taxes in the world. These taxes make the company a tax collector for the government because the extra cost of operation would be passed on to the consumer. As usual, it increases governmental power and penalizes the consumer. It also makes the company less competitive forcing the company to move to lower taxed areas.

There should be more tax deductable charities, locally and nationally, to handle healthcare costs that exceed the person or family's financial capabilities. Healthcare does not need to be dealt with by a large federal government because it becomes impersonal and sub-standard. Associations of people with afflictions and their families can pool their resources for research and drug costs. In the age of ubiquitous communications thru the Internet, they should be able to find one another.

The government could administer healthcare and use taxpayer money while controlling costs but that engenders even more serious problems. Governments, by their nature, always have the problem of incompetence and corruption. The reasons are that there is no competing with government and there is little oversight, which makes for graft and fraud. The government of the United States has been propagandizing imagined problems in the healthcare industry, but the only solutions presented are more control and more money. Because of the recent actions of the United States government, the cost of healthcare has more than doubled and will continue to increase. Doctors are retiring early and medical services are becoming more concentrated. There are also the usual problems with socialism and the tragedy of the commons or any other shared resource, whether it is water or taxpayer money, it is always abused. There are many lawmakers getting kickbacks from the drug companies but they are the shakedown artists, then when caught, they blame the companies.

Attorneys often take advantage of the ambiguity of the outcome of medical procedures. In some cases, the patient or their survivors will receive a large monetary settlement for a real or imagined error on the provider's part. This creates other problems, as it requires the healthcare provider to purchase expensive insurance. One of the biggest costs of healthcare is tests and procedures that are performed to reduce the possibility of litigation. Studies have shown that almost a third of procedures and medicines were unnecessary and even damaging. There is even a pejorative given to trial attorneys practicing this form of law, "ambulance chasers". Some attorneys have made millions with little more than courtroom theatrics. One famous lawyer even had a "supernatural" communication with a fetus.

There are many line items on a hospital bill, not only for tests, but also for hundreds or thousands of dollars for doctors that looked in at a patient or just glanced at their records. Their consulting fee is usually to protect the attending doctor from lawsuits. There are solutions to the legal profession distorting medical practice and driving up costs and at the same time providing oversight. They include such things as having the loser pays for court costs in litigation and tort reform that would limit the awards to the victims or survivors. These reforms would decrease the incidence of litigation and the impact of the legal industry on the medical industry. It would reduce the cost of litigation would allow attorneys for medical organization not to settle but contest huge settlements.

In some cases lawsuits and settlements are warranted because there is a certain amount of actual dishonesty and malpractice. It is usually less expensive to pay a claim than investigate it so it can be considered to be the insurance providers fault for not policing their clients properly. The cost of settlement is just passed along to other medical insurance policy holders. It is the same as allowing someone to have insurance and operate a motorcycle that keeps having accidents. The same medical provider is allowed to practice, injuring and killing patients because no one stops them.

There is no question that the medical profession needs to be more aggressive about policing itself and, if necessary, take away the offender's license to practice. Unfortunately, that works about as well as the legal profession or the government policing itself. In the United States there are too many attorneys but the opposite problem exists in the medical profession. Doctors regularly overlook the mistakes of others. If medical mistakes were considered a disease, it would be the sixth most deadly in the United States. There are few review boards and doctors keep making the same mistakes over and over, costing tens of billions of dollars every year. There are some doctors that have the most wonderful "bedside manner" but destruction and death follows after them wherever they go. There are many economic pressures on medical providers, which set them up for mistakes and lawsuits.

There are solutions to cost and medical mayhem; for instance, doctors and hospitals should have checklists. Airlines have them for everything, but they also have an incredible safety record. In procedures, there needs to be certainty that everything is right before the procedure starts and continues. There needs to be double, even triple checks by those concerned. It would help obviate problems caused by overworked medical staff. If every procedure had a checklist, written by research organizations and funded by insurance companies, there would be far less mistakes. "Is this the correct patient?" "Check!" "The correct procedure?" "Check!" "The correct body part?" "Check!" "Do we have all the tools needed" "Check!" When the procedure is finished: "Are all the instruments and sponges removed from the patient?" and so on.

There should be an occupation that would handle the overview of complex procedures to be sure that it is done correctly. The doctor and medical technicians could do their jobs while the "procedureist" conducts the process similarly to a conductor of an orchestra. He doesn't need to know how to play the violin but only when it needs to be played. This person would oversee the checklist and any divergence to another checklist. They would be paid by lower procedural, insurance and litigation costs or directly by the patient. The doctor, of course, would still have the final say in an emergency situation.

It would be much better for all concerned to increase the odds of success before a medical procedure is done. One way is to use the modern version of word of mouth, on-line ratings and comments. People regularly use the Internet for restaurants but not something as important as medical procedures. Safety of medical providers should be published so that patients can be informed as to the best place to go for a procedure. There are concerns about the privacy of the patient but there is a question about who is being served, the patient or the doctor. Cameras and video recorders are inexpensive and ubiquitous, if the doctor is doing it right, there would be no problem recording the procedure and even allow the patient to have a copy, if desired.

There should be openness; in many cases patients are required to sign a contract that disallows them from publically saying anything bad about the provider. If there is a problem the attorneys for the provider will make the patient's silence part of any settlement. Patients should know what the doctor is putting in their records and if that information is correct. Patients should be allowed keep a copy of their own medical records. If health care providers have a problem with any of this, perhaps one should seek another provider. If there were government regulations involved, it would be worthwhile to see if those laws can be enforced or changed. Unfortunately, in some communities there are few choices and, of course, it is difficult to be discerning with a completely government controlled and restricted system such as in the United Kingdom.

If one looks up ways to reduce the cost of healthcare for themselves they usually include such things as stay healthy or shop around for providers and insurance plans. While these make sense for each individual, it does not help the big picture of healthcare costs trending upward. One good solution that is applicable in the United States and other countries is to have the government stop their quest to take control of the healthcare industry. Costs can not be reduced by adding layers of governmental bureaucracy. One would think if the government were truly concerned about citizen's healthcare and not interested in more power and money they would stop taxing income that went to pay for healthcare. In addition, the government could reduce the taxes on healthcare providers that would be passed along to the consumers.

Health savings accounts or "HSA" is a tax deferred bank account that is used to pay medical expenses from bandages to medicines and major surgery. If one stays healthy quite a lot of money can be put into the account for future illnesses. They also come with an insurance policy that will become active if costs exceed a certain amount. It is basically insuring one's self with a limit on catastrophic expenses. It is certainly a good idea to have some sort of savings account as a buffer to sure poverty. It was a workable system because it put the responsibility for healthcare on the individual. It is presently being eradicated by the Affordable Care Act, which is not very affordable and doesn't supply care.

Another way to reduce the cost of healthcare is not to provide it. The cost of keeping someone alive that is close to death is phenomenal. In the United States it is almost half the cost of all health care. These expenses are passed along to the general population thru the high cost of medical care, insurance companies and the government. Socialist government programs such as in the United Kingdom simply use triage or "death panels" to reduce end of life expenses. If someone that is too elderly and ill that they are having difficulty staying alive on their own treatments are restricted and they are allowed to die. The high cost of keeping them alive for a few extra months is avoided.

The Death Panel method will reduce the overall cost of healthcare. The savings would be passed along to others including the ones that are deemed by the panel to be a good long-term investment. This triage would not apply to someone that has their own resources and wishes to use it to keep themselves alive. Then again, outside of the rich and some socialized countries with honest governments, the only options available are to seek charity or suffer. Your health and life are predicated not solely on your genetics but also your birth circumstances. Individuals need to be allowed to improve their own position in life. It also requires them to be motivated to expand their options.

The Universe has an almost infinite number of possibilities to end our existence and it will always win. We will soon have the capability of molding ourselves to any pattern that is possible. While we have control of our capabilities and eventually evolution, let's have fun with it and see where it can go. There are truly no limits.

Luno

I believe that the only way that the human race is
gonna survive is to start colonizing space and setting
up colonies on the moon, and then space stations.

~ACE FREHLEY

THE OBVIOUS NEXT step for humanity is the colonization of
space. It is not for everyone but a percentage of humanity will participate. We humans are lucky to have the stepping stone to the greater
Universe conveniently located nearby. It is the Moon. It is over one-
fourth the diameter of the Earth. All of the other moons in the Solar
System are thousands of times smaller than their planets. It is clas-
sified as a satellite because the center of mass of the Earth - Moon
system lies about ten percent of the diameter beneath the surface of
the Earth. It creates a noticeable wobble as the Earth and Moon orbit
as seen from space. The Sun's gravitational pull on the Moon is more
than twice the Earth's. The Moon's orbit always falls toward the Sun
not the Earth. All other satellites fall toward their primary.

The surface area of the Moon is fully one fourth of the land area
of the Earth or about the same as North and South America combined. It is almost five times the size of the contiguous United States.

It is big! It is quite dense for a Moon and studies have shown that it has an iron core like the Earth. The Moon is intimately tied to life on earth in many ways including the tides.

The Moon is moving away from the Earth by about four centimeters per year. The Moon was very slightly larger during the dinosaur era. In fifty million years, a blink of an eye in geologic time, the center of mass will be above the Earth's surface and it will become a true planet by definition. It may not be called a planet at this point in time but it certainly acts like one. Some scientists and even the European Space Agency have called the Earth - Moon a dual planet system. It is a bit smaller than Mercury and a bit larger than Pluto.

In so many ways, the Moon is more like a planet. Perhaps, it would be better to give it a name instead of the generic form "moon". The convention in English and many languages uses a capitalized word for the Moon in the Earth's sky and the lower case moon for the generalization. The name for the Earth is similar, in that it also means the ground or soil. One idea would be to give them true names instead of capitalizing the generic terms. A thought would be to use the Esperanto language, the Moon would be Luno and the Earth is Tero. In Latin languages the feminine "la luna" would be generic for all bodies orbiting planets and from Esperanto, "Luno" would be the one in Earth orbit. Note, nouns in Esperanto do not indicate sex because they all end in "o".

The latest theories posit that the Moon was formed from materials blasted from the Earth's crust by the impact of a Mars sized object when it was about hundred million years old. The collision vaporized the material at the impact site and remelted the cooling mantle of the Earth. Initially, the ejected material formed a ring that accreted into the spherical Moon by the force of its own gravity. The theory is given a great deal of credence because the composition of the Moon is nearly identical to the Earth's crust but different than the soil of planet Mars and the asteroid Vesta. The crust of the Moon has been estimated to be about fifty kilometers but there are significant differences from the near side and far side. It may be due to a second much smaller Earth moon or asteroid that impacted the present Moon on the near side. The site is visible as the face of the "man in the Moon".

One theory for the creation of the Moon is that the Pacific Ocean basin is a possible site of an impact and the origin of the lunar material. There is no trace of the impacting body which is somewhere within the Earth. It has mixed with the mantle material after five billion years. The impactor is also thought to have given the Earth its axis tilt, which make the seasons possible. It also decreased the length of a day, that is, increased the rotational speed, which is rather fast for a body its size. The planet Venus, which is about the same size as the Earth rotates on its axis over two hundred times slower and in the opposite direction.

Humans have already been to the Moon. Neil Armstrong stepped onto the lunar surface and he said that it was "one small step for [a] man, one giant leap for mankind." It completed a national objective that was conceived in 1960 during the Eisenhower Administration. It was proposed in 1961 by the U.S. President John F. Kennedy. In a rousing speech, he promised America and the world a landing on the Moon. "I believe that this nation should commit itself to achieving the goal, before this decade is out, of landing a man on the moon and returning him safely to the earth." It took the politically connected and ruthless Lyndon Johnson to pull it off. Kennedy set the course for manned landing before 1970. That was when America was great with greater goals.

American physicist Gerald K. O'Neill proposed, in his book "High Frontiers, Human Colonies in Space" (1977), methods of becoming a space-faring society. The concept, seemingly expensive at first because of the large amount of mass needed to be lifted into lunar orbit, becomes less expensive once analyzed. It can be difficult to build in a weightless environment but is easier when there is some gravity to hold things stable. He imagined factories on the Moon that would build prefabricated parts to be launched into lunar orbit. He also imagined that ten thousand people would be living in space by the year 1990.

O'Neill may have overlooked a key part of a plan for the colonization of space and that is the colonization of the Moon itself. He wanted to build factories on the Moon and looked at it as an industrial complex, and did not consider it as a potential home for billions of people. O'Neill was concerned about bone and muscle loss in lower gravity. There is no doubt that exercise and drugs including fish oil would mitigate such problems. There might not be a problem at all if one had no intention to return to the Earth.

There have been many plans to colonize the Moon but the only commitment that has been made recently was by Vladimir Putin. He said that Russia would begin the effort to have a colony on the Moon in 2014 and to be in place by 2030. Since the Russian Luna 1 in 1959, the United States, Japan, India, China, NASA and the ESA have all sent spacecraft to the Moon. Several nations on Earth have an industrial infrastructure that could support a manned lunar colonization program, given the political will. The list would include the United States, the European Union, Russia, India, China, Japan, Germany, United Kingdom, France, Italy and South Africa. It would be wonderful if there were an international effort but several competing groups would assure success.

The lack of an atmosphere and lower surface gravity are the two most important natural resources on the Moon. The lack of an atmosphere would give lunar colonists access to undiluted solar power and the low surface gravity would give them inexpensive access to space. The near vacuum on the lunar surface makes it cost effective to use electromagnetic launchers to push mass into orbit or anywhere else. On the Earth, the escape velocity is eleven kilometers per second, on the Moon it is two and a half kilometers per second. When air resistance is included with the energy required for an Earth launch, a lunar launch is less than one-fifth the energy. Placing objects into lunar orbit would only need a launch speed of about five thousand kilometers per hour.

Humans would live longer in the lower gravity; a sixty-kilogram person on Earth would weigh about ten kilograms on the Moon. The strain on the heart and other organs would be much less. Broken hips from falls would no longer be a problem unless the fall was from a great height. Breaking a hip on Earth is usually caused by a twisting fall from less than one meter. To land with the same force on the Moon the fall must be from six meters and would take almost three seconds. There would be more than enough time to right oneself before damage was done.

Power generation would be a primary concern to colonize the Moon. The lunar surface receives thirteen thousand Terawatts of power from the sun. By 2050, humanity will need twenty Terawatts of power, a mere two tenths of a percent of solar power available on the Moon. A collection belt around the equator of the moon fifty kilometers wide could provide ALL the power for humanity on the Earth and the Moon and spacecraft to travel in between. The Shimizu Corporation has already done the engineering studies and it could be built as needed.

The power would be generated from solar photovoltaic panels made from mostly silicon and aluminum constructed on the Moon with locally derived materials. The panels could also use a simple heat transfer device that would use sunlight to heat ammonia, methane, carbon dioxide or other working fluid into a high-pressure gas to drive turbines. The temperature differential between the sun and shade is about 250 degrees Celsius, more than enough for a heat engine. Large inexpensive mirrors made of aluminum could track the sun to concentrate the power and increase the temperature differential. There is certainly plenty of energy and all it would take an engineering study to determine the most efficient way to extract it. The sale of electrical energy would finance much of the lunar operations once the system is even partially operational. Energy could be beamed directly to receivers in Lunar or Earth orbit where it could be used for operations. It could then be beamed to the Earth's surface from a geo stationary orbit.

There are methods to obtain large quantities of breathable air. Oxygen is not the problem because the crust of the Moon is, by weight, almost half oxygen. The abundant energy available on the Moon would make it cost effective to extract it, not only for use by living things but also to be used as rocket propellant. Nitrogen, the largest component of air on the Earth, is also available on the moon but in a smaller quantity and can be extracted from lunar materials. It would serve the same purpose as on the Earth to mitigate the oxidizing effects of oxygen and would provide higher air pressure to support overhead structures. It would also be available from captured comets as frozen ammonia.

It would be worthwhile to free some of the oxygen from the lunar soil to create an atmosphere on the Moon. Even rarified, an atmosphere would provide a great deal of protection from micrometeorites, solar wind and cosmic rays. Particles coming in perpendicular to the surface would not have much atmosphere to slow them down. Nevertheless, the majority of particles that would come from any other angle would have considerably more atmosphere to travel thru and would be slowed down, vaporized and scattered before they hit the surface.

The solar wind will eventually blow away any atmosphere but there is a limit as to the maximum amount that can be lost per unit of time no matter how dense the atmosphere. The effect, named after NASA scientist Richard Vondrak, is about a trillionth the sea level atmospheric pressure on Earth. The atmosphere would be sustained by adding gas at the rate of one hundred kilograms per second. There is abundant oxygen on the lunar surface to create an atmosphere. Factories releasing oxygen from lunar soil using solar power would be built to replenish the atmosphere constantly. Eventually highly modified organisms can be engineered to wring the oxygen out of lunar soil but the process would need to and cost less than a chemical process. Manufacturing an atmosphere would be one of the later stages of colonization.

There are vast quantities of metals and other construction materials in the lunar soil so that they would not need to be brought up from the Earth. Concrete can be made from lunar rocks altho special techniques would need to be developed on the airless lunar surface. Water can be mixed with other materials and cast like concrete and allowed to freeze. Ice is a good insulator and in a reinforced solid form can be quite strong. There are also carbon and nitrogen present in quantities plus all of the other elements vital for life and used for industry. Some raw materials may need to be transported from the Earth or easier, from the asteroid belt. There may be much more, deep below the lunar surface, that can be mined but that will require on site prospecting.

There is the problem of the availability of water that can be solved in several inexpensive ways. Firstly, there are billions of tons of water, as ice, that has already been discovered on the Moon. Several missions to the moon have discovered a large amount of hydrogen, which indicates water, in deep craters. There have been computer simulations that indicate that over ten thousand square kilometers of the lunar surface receives no sunlight. These areas would contain a great deal of water as ice. There are vastly more billions of tons trapped as hydrates in the depths of lunar soil that would only take heat to release. The Stone Aerospace Corporation has done the engineering and the business plan to use this water to provide fuel for low Earth orbit -Moon spacecraft.

Highly compressed hydrogen from the Earth can be inexpensively sent to orbit with ballistic launchers to meet with vehicles launched from the Moon. They would then return to the Moon and the hydrogen combined with the oxygen that is so plentiful in lunar soil. One ton of hydrogen combined with oxygen would make nine tons of water with the release of a great deal of heat. Vast amounts of hydrogen can also be captured from the solar wind.

The trajectory of comets can be changed with solar powered electric rockets. They would be moved into lunar orbit, broken up and directed to an impact site on the Moon. The comet would also be a source of nitrogen and carbon in the form of ammonia. The cost of the colonization project would be ameliorated by the fact that many of the primary raw materials such as oxygen, silicon, iron, calcium, aluminum, magnesium and titanium are in abundance on the moon. Hydrogen, carbon and nitrogen, needed by living things, are also available but as the lunar population expands more can be harvested, again, from comets, in the form of water, carbon dioxide and ammonia. It would be easier and far less expensive than launching from the Earth. A supply of water and air for the moon is certainly doable and inexpensive even with current technology.

The problem of how to obtain enough material on site to start up a colony to survive indefinitely on the Moon is not a difficult one. Shipments will be one way from the Earth while machinery for local production of power, air, water, food and shelter are being set up. Power generation facilities can be expanded to begin sending power for use in Earth orbit or to downlink stations in geosynchronous orbit around the Earth. The power would be used to make construction materials locally on the Moon plus move cargo back and forth between Earth orbit and the Moon. Again, facilities in Earth orbit would be cheaper to build on the Moon. Near Earth space could be colonized by space stations and orbital habitats.

The first Moon landing occurred on the 20th of July 1969. It is saddening to think that the first man to set foot on the Moon, Neil Armstrong, has passed away and no humans have returned to the Moon since December 1972. There was an attempt to reinstate a less expensive lunar program that would result in a permanent presence on the moon by President G. W. Bush in 2004 but it was cancelled by Barack Obama in 2011. Again, Vladimir Putin announced that Russia will have a permanent settlement on the Moon by 2040. The Chinese are planning a lunar landing before 2030. The United States has no coherent lunar program.

Abode

"We can continue to try and clean up the gutters all over the world and spend all of our resources looking at just the dirty spots and trying to make them clean. Or we can lift our eyes up and look into the skies and move forward in an evolutionary way."

~ BUZZ ALDRIN

THE ENGINEERING AND construction of large habitable open spaces underground on the Moon need not be difficult. The largest natural open area underground on Earth is the Son Doong cave in Vietnam. It is two hundred meters high, one hundred fifty meters wide, and nine kilometers long. Most caves on Earth form by water flowing, making it unlikely that there are any natural caves on the Moon. The gravity on the Moon is one sixth of the Earth, so a self-supporting man made cave could be six times these dimensions or a kilometer high and kilometer wide. If supports and structural strength were added, it could far larger. For comparison, Manhattan Island averages about three kilometers wide and about twenty kilometers long. The tallest building on Earth is the Burj Khlifa over eight hundred meters tall; an equivalent engineering feat on the Moon would be almost five kilometers.

The Shackleton crater, named after the Antarctic explorer, is located at the lunar south pole. It has been studied a great deal and would make an ideal first settlement. It is a circular crater that is over twenty kilometers across and over four kilometers deep, twice as deep as the Grand Canyon. The rotational axis of the Moon actually lies within the crater so it has not seen sunlight in hundreds of millions of years. The depths of the crater are in eternal darkness with known large quantities of mineral ice. It has a high crater wall that receives constant solar energy as the Moon rotates about its axis. The crater has a large amount of solar power available that would be collected by mirrors on movable mounts. They would rotate in the opposite direction at the same speed as the lunar day - night cycle or every twenty-nine Earth days. There is water and lots of energy, a paradise indeed!

The Shackleton crater is known to have large deposits of ice that could be used for fuel by using solar power or to crack the water into hydrogen and oxygen. The hydrogen and oxygen could be recombined in a rocket engine for trips to the Earth or other parts of the Solar system. As soon as they can be built, chemical rockets would be replaced by magnetic launchers. The facilities at Shackleton would "bootstrap" colonization, which would become more economical as the frequency of round trip travel between the Earth and Moon increases and factories have been built.

Initially, unmanned missions to the Moon could set up habitats and have supplies ready for colonists to arrive. It could be done inexpensively using cost effective launching systems. The habitats on the Moon would be resupplied from the Earth in the beginning, as they are in Antarctic. If some of the colonists wish to return to the Earth or have products shipped from the Moon back to the Earth, the cost of the return trip is much less than the trip from the Earth. If you have seen videos of the lunar missions from the 1970's you saw that it was a small rocket on the Lunar Lander that launched the astronauts back into lunar orbit.

The lunar colonies would be made a pleasant place to live. There would be hydroponics farms to grow algae and other plants for air renewal and food. They would thrive on cheap energy that would power solar spectrum lamps and use recycled biological materials. The large underground open areas could be used to cultivate crops in soil and even forests. The colonists would take some species of animals with them for food altho, by this time, plants would have been modified to have almost any flavor and texture desired. The lunar colonists would have fish, chicken, turkey, ducks and some mammals such as sheep, rabbits, goats, and guinea pigs. It would seem that chickens would be common, but they would need to have their wings clipped, because on the Moon they would be able to fly. Of course, we would have our cats, dogs, songbirds and other pets that would need to be adjusted to the lesser gravity.

The biota could either be tightly controlled or allowed to be free to be imported wild from the Earth. It would need to include digestive and skin bacteria, because animals require their symbiotes for proper health. Insects would be selected for their benefits and beauty but would need tight control. Birds, reptiles and mammals would be easier to control with sterilization if needed. If there were a problem with the contamination of any of the colonies by harmful species, it could be abandoned and opened to the vacuum of space for a period of time. It would also be sterilized by heating to about one hundred twenty Celsius, or ultraviolet lamps. There could be organisms modified for a lunar life style or even artificial organisms. Different communities could set their own rules.

Living on the Moon could be like living in one of the world's giant shopping malls with large open spaces, plants and lots of color. The largest in the United States is the Mall of America in Minneapolis with almost half a million square meters of floor space. Another, designed as a one stop destination in the harsh winters, is the largest in the

Western Hemisphere, the West Edmonton Mall in Alberta, Canada with over half a million square meters. About the same size, and the largest shopping Mall in Europe, is the Cevahir in Istanbul, Turkey. The largest mall in the world in 2012 is the South China Dongguan Mall located near Hong Kong.

These large malls are truly cities unto themselves. The temperature and humidity inside is regulated to be like a comfortable cool spring day. They can be built in some of the most inhospitable places on Earth given enough inexpensive energy. Dubai, a hot, dry desert kingdom has been turned into one of the more comfortable albeit one of the more expensive places to live. There are more shopping malls in hot, steamy Asia including several in China, Malaysia, India, Indonesia, Philippines and Iran.

Many of these Meccas of capitalism have hotels and apartments attached and the same would be the case on the Moon, perhaps even more so. There would be many restaurants, because people living on the Moon would want to return to the more normal custom of not cooking at home except for, perhaps, a small microwave oven. They would go to one of the many restaurants that would have cuisine from any of the cultures on Earth made from locally grown foods. They would probably also have things that have not been tried on the Earth.

The tunnels, caverns and craters on the Moon would be commodious as a living habitat; there would be cities that would make Shanghai or Mexico City seen small. They could support huge populations that would work in the mines, manufacturing and in space. The highly educated population would be healthy and long living because harmful diseases and parasites would not be imported from the Earth. There would be high-speed subways between population centers and industrial and farming areas.

There are so many reasons to send humans to the Moon that volumes and volumes have been written about it. There are over fifty thousand books with Moon in the title on Amazon alone. The importance of the Moon as the future home of the largest part of humanity for the next few centuries and the gateway to the Universe can't be overstated. Towns and cities could be built in areas with harsh climates on the Earth if there is inexpensive energy available and that certainly could be done. Nevertheless, the goal at this point in time must also be to move people off of the Earth and expand the realm of humanity.

Migration to the Moon would allow a huge expansion of the number of humans as it could support a far larger population than the Earth. There is no environment to damage only to create. The lunar surface and the Sun could provide more than enough power and the vast majority of the raw materials. If the Moon had a population of, for example, seven billion people or the current population of the Earth, it would have less population density than Italy, which no one would deny is a delightful place to live. Huge tunnels and caverns could be built to resemble that of a Tuscan town or any other town. There would be high-speed trains built in tunnels connecting communities around the Moon.

Consider the possibility that a mere one five percent of the surface of the Moon were mined, an area the size of Mexico or three times the size of France. Additionally, those tunnels and voids were to be made available as living space. Let us further assume a population density the same as the lovely city of Paris, France. The Moon could have a population of about forty billion, almost six times the present population of the Earth. The Earth could become a park; people would save up to visit the ancestral homeland but they would have to be quite fit and work out because they will be six times heavier. The elderly on the Moon may never be able to go back to the Earth and only be able to visit only by video. Friends and relatives that live on Earth could visit them on the Moon much as they now visit retirement communities in Florida and Arizona.

The Moon is ideal to support a large population. In fact, the low gravity, no atmosphere and lack of an indigenous population (or

anything living) make the Moon perfect for industry and colonization. Current estimates of the human carrying capacity of the Earth,
with a reasonable standard of living, are between sixteen and forty
billion people with varying amounts of damage to the environment.
The carrying capacity range depends upon how much environmental
damage could be tolerated. The Moon doesn't have a living ecology to
be concerned about. All that is needed is easily obtainable construction materials, air and water and those are aplenty with inexpensive
energy. A population of ten times the Earth would be possible.

The Biosphere project of the University of Arizona was initiated
in 1987 as an experiment to create an artificial self-sustaining environment. The project originated with a great deal of idealism that
overshadowed cold hard engineering. It had huge glass roofs for sunlight and, inside, different habitats or biomes were created. There
was a desert, savannah, rain forest, wetlands, ocean and a coral reef.
The attempt was to make the Biosphere completely recyclable, perhaps an impossible task. It was set up, it seems, less for science and
more for a new age religious experience for environmentalists. There
were problems caused by the impractical idealism of the creators.
The biosphere inhabitants were on restricted diets making them irri-
table and low energy. The concrete walls and floor absorbed carbon
dioxide. Plants would die and there were constant insect infestations
because insecticide was not allowed. Everything was to be recycled;
later in the experiment outside air was used so that the project would
not be a complete failure. It did work once it was determined that
some raw materials were needed from time to time. It proved once
again, that just about anything is possible with enough energy even
tho in this case the energy was natural gas. The Biosphere facility is
still in use by the University of Arizona.

The Institute of Biophysics in Soviet Russia had a similar but
more modest project on a tighter budget called Bios3. It was more
scientific and less idealistic than the Biosphere project. It used
xenon lamps to provide artificial sunlight as could be used on a

spacecraft or the Moon. It was used to test closed recycling systems to support humans. One of the important discoveries was that the average human needs about eight square meters of chlorella algae to replenish the air with oxygen thru photosynthesis. The facility is still operation and is now used in cooperation with European Space Agency.

On the Lunar colonies, humans would live in a shirtsleeve (no pressure suits) environment of tunnels, caverns and roofed over craters. Tunnels would be the result of mining operations that would be dug into the lunar regolith. These underground open spaces could be large, with buildings constructed in the open spaces and into the walls of the caverns. Mining operations would create soil that would be mixed with biological byproducts to create living soil. There is plenty of room to build these open spaces; the crust of the Moon is quite thick for its size. It averages fifty kilometers, even thicker than the larger Earth, which averages ten kilometers.

Craters could be roofed over by a framework of aluminum, which is abundant on the Moon. The frame would be spanned by tiles of painted ice... yes, ice. On the Moon, water is a mineral if kept out of the sun even if by a thin layer of foil or paint. The crater roofs would be held up by air pressure and kilometer tall pylons or buildings. These underground designs would keep the air in and micrometeorites and cosmic rays out. Meteors would not be a problem as those large enough to be a problem would be detected by a vigilant radar system and destroyed by particle beams or rail guns. Again, these are designs that can be accomplished easily by a large nation or small but committed one or even a large corporation.

The tunnels and caverns would have sunlight spectral lamps overhead that could be turned on and off to match the twenty-four hour day-night cycle of the Earth and not the month long "day" of the Moon. The ceiling of the open and farming areas would be lit up by banks of lamps. There could be dimmable lamps or even a bank of lights moving on a track to simulate the Sun, as it would appear on Earth. There would be catwalks or compressed air powered flying machines to maintain lighting and sprinkler systems.

Populated areas could be lit by high power lights being reflected from the ceiling. Creative lighting and projection techniques could make it look like any sort of sky on Earth or something even more interesting like a planetarium. Beneath the lamp-lit tunnels and domes there could be farms and cities thriving on cheap energy and recycled materials. It would be a pleasant place with fantastic architecture because of the low gravity with gardens and fountains everywhere.

Sprinkler systems could not only be used in case of fire but for artificial rain. There can be artificially created weather and that can be anything desired. A bit of ozone could be added to the air to give the same smell as a thunderstorm on the Earth. Caverns could have rain to clean off surfaces and snow for winter sports. Rain and snow would drift down at one sixth the speed of the Earth; a gentle rain would be gentle. It would be used to cleanse the habitat to be recycled thru the ponds and streams that would be dotted around the area. Rain could be produced on a schedule to keep everything green and clean in the cavern. The floors and walls of the caverns would be sealed to prevent air and water from seeping out, perhaps coated with silicone foam manufactured from the easily available silicon and oxygen. If there were any leaks, they would be inexpensively repaired and the air replaced. The gardens and trees in the caverns would contribute to the oxygen recycling facilities.

Streams would be part of the sanitation system with water runoff draining into small lakes where the water could be filtered and recycled. Forests would be grown to recycle the air and provide construction materials. Buildings can be made of wood with no worry of termites. Cities would grow inside the huge caverns. Farming under artificial lights would become so efficient that food could be exported to other colonies and even the Earth. There could be rivers that would snake through the tunnels that could also collect any pollutants that would then be filtered and returned to the source.

Caverns could specialize in producing various climates. There could be an area for deserts and another for winter sports. Snow could be made using the sprinkler systems and skiing could be done by novices on the steepest piste. Images could be projected on the roof of the cavern to give the appearance of a larger area and display any type of weather condition.

An object on the Earth, in one second, would fall about five meters. In order to strike the ground with the same force on the Moon as that one-second fall on Earth, you would need to fall from almost thirty meters and it would take six seconds. On the Moon a human could fly with little or no mechanical assistance, not glide as on Earth but using human muscles to propel them in actual flight. On Earth, the most efficient designs of human powered flying machines require, at least, five hundred watts. That is something even the best athlete would have a difficult time doing. On the Moon less than one hundred watts is needed, well within the range of a healthy young human. The Moon would truly be a lovely place to live.

The sale of plentiful power and a tourist industry would pay for ongoing colonization. The question is then, how to ramp up to move supplies and humans to the Moon inexpensively? These are actually two different questions. Humans can be launched but with a force not much more than three times Earth gravity. Supplies and equipment can be launched with a force much greater than humans could tolerate. The colonization of the Moon will be a magnificent project with adventures and stories that would be told and dramatized far into the future.

Launch

"The dinosaurs became extinct because they didn't have a space program. And if we become extinct because we don't have a space program, it'll serve us right!"

~LARRY NIVEN, QUOTED BY ARTHUR CLARKE IN AN INTERVIEW AT SPACE.COM, 2001

THE DREAM OF moving populations off the planet does not mean much unless it can actually be done and inexpensively. We now fly around the globe on giant aircraft that can carry hundreds of people in relative comfort. On average, there are about a million people in the sky at any given time. That is something that would have been whimsy in 1800 and at the edge of possibility in 1900. Flying to another city is in the price range of the average working person living the developed world. The same will apply to moving large numbers of people off the planet; demand and the economics will drive the price down.

The goal is shift to people and cargo from the Earth to the Moon and return, economically. The biggest and most expensive leap is moving off of the Earth to low Earth orbit or LEO. It becomes easier and much less expensive after that. Surprisingly, once we make the leap to the Moon, it will be much easier to build and resupply LEO facilities from manufacturing plants on the Moon.

Over a billion people fly on aircraft every year on about twenty million flights. If a launch rate of rockets to the Moon were to occur one thousandth as often, a million people could make the trip in one year. If ten percent as often, the entire human population of the Earth could be moved to the Moon in less than a century. As technology and launch capacity increases, traffic to the Moon would multiply. The Earth could return to its "natural" state, whatever that would be. The population of the Earth could be reduced to the dream of self-styled environmentalists and "progressives". That is, reduced to about five hundred million people without resorting to genocide, not that they have been historically troubled by it.

One of the most successful launch systems was the Saturn V built by the United States. It was used for the Apollo Moon missions from 1969 to 1973 and was the most powerful rocket that has ever been built. It could deliver over one hundred tons, the same as six Space Shuttles, to LEO or almost fifty tons to lunar orbit. It was a multistage rocket, built to take three passengers and a lunar lander, on a single launch, to the Moon and return the passengers to Earth. It was used to get twenty four people to the Moon and twelve of them actually walked on it.

The United States space program was started with several hundred rocket engineers and technicians including Wernher von Braun. He was one of the leading engineers who developed the rocket program for Nazi Germany and became the lead engineer for NASA and the Apollo Moon landing project. The first space station, Skylab, was launched by the last Saturn V in 1973. It was allowed to fall back to the Earth in 1979 because of the vast sums that were to be needed for the space shuttle.

The manufacturing of the Saturn V was stopped because of the cost and the debt incurred by the Vietnam War. The plans are still available on microfilm. It was a grand plan whose primary goal was propaganda. When the propaganda battle with the Soviet Union was won, it was shut down. There are many who don't even believe that humans have walked on the Moon, which is sad and telling of the state of society and the trust of government.

Unfortunately, there are more political problems than technological problems in having a transportation system to space and the Moon. The Space Shuttle was a far more expensive proposition than the Apollo lunar missions. It was sold to the American people as an inexpensive and reliable space vehicle. It was an engineering marvel but it turned out that it was neither inexpensive nor reliable. It was sold to a willing congress as having fifty missions per year but due to huge cost overruns the most that it ever managed was nine.

Over the 135 Space Shuttle launches from 1981 to 2011 the program cost more, adjusted for inflation, than the Apollo Moon missions, the Manhattan project to build the first atomic bomb and the Panama Canal, combined. It could carry a load of about twenty tons, one-fifth of the capacity of the Saturn V and one tenth of a Boeing 747 aircraft, to LEO. It had an inflation-adjusted cost of sixty thousand dollars per kilogram. The contemporary Soviet / Russian Proton rocket was less than one-tenth the cost per kilogram delivered to LEO. The Soviets had a similar shuttle program, called Buran or Blizzard; it was scrapped during the collapse of the Soviet Union but there are efforts to revise it. There are much less expensive ways into Earth orbit and more being developed.

The Shuttle program cost so much that NASA, forced by Congress to support it, had to scrap plans for almost every other endeavor in space. It was not designed to be a heavy lift vehicle but to transport humans into space and return. It was built before it was needed and a disaster to the manned space program, but that's politics. The saving grace for the extremely expensive Shuttle was the Hubble Telescope. The Hubble Telescope would have been a miserable failure, but the Shuttle and billions of dollars of added cost managed to save the day.

The story of the Hubble and the mirror being ground incorrectly is a story of incompetence and cover-your-ass at the highest levels.

The Bush administration approved a more economical return to the Moon program. The Constellation Program would use an assortment of manned and unmanned rockets. The Ares I was for manned launches, designed with the most safety using the Shuttle solid rocket booster as the first stage and liquid fuel upper stages. It could deliver up to six people to Low Earth orbit. The capsule could also return humans safely to Earth using the tried and true system of an ablative heat shield used for early space flights including the Apollo program. The Ares V is a heavy lift multistage rocket that would use two of the solid rocket boosters plus a Shuttle type tank and engines. It was to be unmanned and have a lifting capacity of almost two hundred tons to Low Earth orbit and sixty tons to the Moon. The cost of establishing a lunar colony would have been considerably less than the Space Shuttle program.

The Obama administration has shut down the more economical return to the Moon program and much of NASA funding. This was quite surprising as he and his Democrat Congress were certainly not shy about spending on much of anything else. It was quite short-sighted because it will take a great deal of money and effort to reassemble the teams that could have gotten it done. It has delayed an American lunar return by another decade or more. The cities and towns around Cape Canaveral are ghost towns and American rocket scientists are looking for employment with military contractors and overseas. He has asked NASA to plan an unmanned rocket to an asteroid. Some believe the money would be far better spent on a permanent human presence in space.

It will take private enterprise a good deal of time and money to get to the Moon. It would help considerably if there were tax incentives and subsides for the development of private space technology. Unfortunately, in the United States, the Obama government has created a permanent crisis environment so that is unlikely to happen.

The way things are looking, an American that wants to go to the Moon in the future will have to obtain a Russian or Chinese visa.

There are several engineering problems or steps involved in moving people reliably to the Moon and back and inexpensively enough to allow for commerce. The first step is propelling the vehicle to above the Earth's thick lower atmosphere with minimum damage. The vehicle uses a great deal of fuel as it moves thru the lower atmosphere to overcome air resistance. It must also be able to handle the turbulence of speeding thru a fluid and that requires a well engineered compromise design that is strong but lightweight. The problem of safely lifting through the atmosphere can be and has been solved by booster rockets, aircraft and even balloons. Ideally, they would lift the vehicle to a height of sixteen kilometers, leaving ninety percent of the atmosphere behind.

There has been much success using aircraft and balloon launching platforms. The rocket is lifted to a predetermined height then it is dropped so that it will be far enough away from the lifting vehicle when the rocket engine fires. There are aircraft big enough to carry a small rocket to an altitude of about eight kilometers, then the rocket engine fires. The rocket continues to its destination and the lifting vehicle then returns to the airport and could refuel and pick up another rocket for the next launch.

The payloads of these air-launched rockets are generally small but they could meet in low Earth Orbit to be assembled into larger systems. It could be an inexpensive way to space; there are several companies including Richard Branson's Virgin Galactic are developing such systems. The Virgin system is proposed to carry about two hundred kilograms to LEO at a cost of less than ten thousand dollars per kilogram. A successful test launch occurred in April 2013. Another company, Stratolaunch Systems will test in 2016, an aircraft that uses six Boeing 747 engines to lift a rocket that would be capable to place six tons into low Earth orbit. It is the same payload as the now defunct Space Shuttle but at a fraction of the cost.

The second step and the biggest, is gaining enough velocity to achieve orbit, which becomes easier once the vehicle is above the atmosphere. About eight kilometers per second velocity is required to achieve a low Earth orbit of one hundred sixty kilometers. If the payload does not have more than this critical velocity, it will fall back to Earth on a ballistic trajectory. Multistage rockets have a large first stage that will lift the payload high out of the atmosphere. The second stage rocket then ignites and adds enough velocity to make it into orbit. The first stage would not have enough speed; it is designed to fall back to the Earth on a predetermined trajectory.

There are several powerful launch vehicles available at this time. One is the Boeing Delta IV heavy that can put almost thirty tons into LEO, thirteen tons into geosynchronous orbit or nine tons into Earth escape orbit. The cost of delivering material to the Moon would be about seventeen thousand dollars per kilogram. Using these rockets and multiple launches, it would be about two billion dollars to move one hundred tons of material to lunar orbit. The engineering the packages, manned launches and soft landing the equipment and personnel that would be needed for the lunar operation would be added to the total cost.

There are other powerful launch vehicles that have been developed by various nations that could be even more cost effective. They could also be enlisted in the Moon colonization project. For example, the Russian Krunichev Proton-M, Soyuz and Angara series, the European Space Agency Arianne 5, the Japanese Mitsubishi H2B and the Chinese CZ (Changzheng or Long March) series of rockets, the Ukranian Zenit and the Indian GSLV.

The Falcon Heavy launch system is being privately developed by Space-X, founded by Paypal entrepreneur Elon Musk. It will be the most powerful rocket since the Saturn V was used on the Apollo Moon landings. It will have the ability to put fifty tons, about the same as two shuttle launches, into low Earth orbit or sixteen tons into lunar orbit. The cost of launch is projected to be as low as twenty five hundred dollars per kilogram to low Earth orbit or eight thousand per kilogram into lunar orbit. It would be competitive with other launch systems, as it was designed to be comparatively simple and reliable. Space-X is now doing resupply missions to the International Space Station.

It would make sense to use an existing technology of cheaper, more reliable launch vehicles with multiple launches. They would rendezvous in low Earth orbit to be assembled in space as a lunar landing system. Enough of these launches, manned and unmanned, could send enough material to the Moon to build self-sustaining systems. Human colonists could then follow on later missions. This is technology that is now off-the-shelf that could be brought to bear on the goal of a human colony on the Moon within a few years. Chemical rockets with assembly line construction techniques and multiple launches could reduce the cost to Low Earth Orbit to less than a thousand dollars per kilogram.

If inexpensive rockets were mass-produced and launched at, perhaps, a rate of one or more per day a large space station or colony on the moon could be quickly built. There was a paper written in 1993 by John Walker "A Rocket a Day Keeps the High Costs Away". In it, he explained how costs could be considerably reduced by using inexpensive mass produced vehicles. The costs were extrapolated from the Nazi German production of V2 rockets during World War Two. An intelligence analyst at the time determined that using slave labor; the Mittlewerk plant could have produced about a thousand V2 rockets per month. That was over seventy years ago and was done while being bombed by the allies!

If rockets were mass produced, the cost of launches could be reduced by a factor of ten or more. It could even be a two stage device with the spent first stage being returned to the ground and the factory for refurbishing. The entire budget would be less than two billion U.S. dollars per year. This amount is within ten percent of the military budget of most modern countries including Poland

and Algeria. It is a tiny fraction of the bloated military budget of the United States as well as China and Russia. The technology is there all that is needed is the resolve.

The third step is Earth to the Moon. During the Apollo missions a parking orbit around the Earth was used to check that the spacecraft made it thru the launch with no damage and was prepared to head for the Moon. The rocket of the third stage was fired to send the payload to a lunar orbit. If the rocket is powerful enough it can go directly from an Earth launch directly to lunar orbit.

This step is not only to orbit the Moon but to anywhere in the Solar System. Adding a mere three kilometers per second would free the vehicle from Earth's gravity. Adding yet another five kilometers per second to the velocity of the vehicle can propel it all the way to orbit around Saturn. A gravity assist boost from Jupiter could propel a vehicle to the outer planets or even out of the solar system.

The fourth step is landing on the Moon, which is different than the Earth because there is no atmosphere to slow the vehicle and a parachute can't be used. Rockets must be used to slow the vehicle below lunar orbital speed; it will then drop along a ballistic arc to the surface. Using orbital mechanics, a computer can accurately drop it in the right place. It would then use rockets to slow to a soft landing. It could also land similar to an aircraft on Earth and use magnetic fields to slow it down. The Moon has less the gravity than the Earth so considerably less power is needed for lunar landing and launches.

The fifth step is launching from the Moon but, again, because of the lower gravity, it is much easier than the Earth. To return to Earth a much smaller chemical rocket can be used. The fuel could be brought up from the Earth or better, made from local water on the Moon by cracking water into oxygen and hydrogen. Once the infrastructure is in place, a solar powered electric launcher would be built for about the same cost of building an airport. This device could easily provide the thrust to place a payload in lunar or Earth orbit. The same launcher could be used to propel vehicles to anywhere in the solar system.

The sixth step is to return safely to the Earth from orbit. The vehicle must lose orbital velocity before it can land. Currently, there are special maneuvers performed and heat shields used to reduce the speed by changing the kinetic energy to heat. A mass produced shuttle type vehicle could also be used that would glide to a landing at a specially equipped airport. This all known technology that is currently in use. Given the availability of inexpensive materials on the Moon, these crossings would become routine.

The path is clear and there are many ways; all it takes is the will. Considering the vast riches that have been squandered for the benefit of the corrupt and the insanity of war, is it not time to move all humanity forward? There are fortunes to be made as humanity spreads out into space that would make the gross domestic product of the entire planet Earth pale in comparison. We had the technology to send a colony to the Moon in the1960's we certainly can do it now.

Highway

"There are so many benefits to be derived from space exploration and exploitation; why not take, what seems to me, the only chance of escaping what is otherwise the sure destruction of all that humanity has struggled to achieve for fifty thousand years?"

~Isaac Asimov

ROCKETS ARE GENERALLY launched to the east to get a boost from the Earth's rotation. In addition, there are better places to launch rockets than Cape Canaveral in Florida and Baikonur in Kazakhstan. The launch site for the European Space Agency in Korou, Guiana is much closer to the equator so that it can take advantage of the increased rotational speed of the Earth. All things being equal, a launch from an equatorial site would have twelve percent more velocity than the Cape and thirty percent more than Baikonur for the same payload.

One of the sweet spots to launch rockets is Korou but there is another, Mont Chimborazo in Ecuador; a six kilometer high mountain located on the equator. The summit is the point on the surface of the Earth that is farthest from the center. A magnetic levitation track up the side of Chimborazo could accelerate a large rocket, combined with the Earth's rotational speed to well over ten percent of the required velocity to reach low Earth orbit. At the peak of the mountain, the vehicle would lift off of the track and be thru the densest part of the atmosphere and provide a large savings in fuel. At that point, the rocket engine would fire to continue the launch. The launcher would require a large investment in infrastructure but it and other high volume systems would eventually be needed. They would pay for themselves with an increase in traffic.

A system was being worked on in the late 1950's that could have gotten a human colony on the Moon before 1980: the Orion type atomic spacecraft. This Orion is the same name but not the same vehicle as the President Bush initiated project. This type of spacecraft was designed during the so-called Cold War (propaganda not bullets) between the United States and the Soviet Union. Orion was a design for lifting extremely large masses into orbit and beyond. The concept was to detonate small yield atomic bombs outside the spacecraft to push against a pusher plate. The detonations were to be less than one percent of the size of the Nagasaki bomb, which was actually quite small compared to those produced during the cold war. It would be a shaped explosion to maximize the force against the pusher plate and would give the spaceship an enormous amount of thrust.

There have been subsequent design improvements that would use solid rocket boosters similar to the Space Shuttle. The boosters could lift the vehicle out of the lower atmosphere before the first detonation. After reaching a height of about forty kilometers, the boosters would drop off to be returned to the Earth and recycled. The detonations would then begin and accelerate the vehicle to orbital or trans-lunar velocity. The bombs would be detonated in succession at a rate of about two per second, keeping the craft accelerating. Depending upon number and rapidity of detonations, huge payloads could have been sent to the Moon from a direct launch on the Earth. The sonic vibrations of the detonations would travel thru the craft, making the ride in the atomic spaceship sound similar old steam locomotive chugging along.

The smallest design would have been capable of putting three hundred tons into low Earth Orbit and almost two hundred tons to a soft landing on the Moon. There was a design for an even larger Orion type atomic rocket with a launch mass of ten thousand tons. It would have the capability to put over eight thousand tons of payload into low Earth orbit. It would also be capable of soft landing almost six thousand tons on the Moon or the same as two hundred and fifty fully loaded semi-trailers. A fully equipped and populated lunar colony in a single launch! It would have jump-started humanity into being a space faring society.

The project was scrapped because of wildly exaggerated fears of nuclear fallout and finally, the test ban treaty of 1963. One must keep in mind that it was designed and engineered with the technology available more than half a century ago. Using computer modeling and the more advanced materials designs available today, it would be even more safe and efficient.

There is a technology using a large cannon type device to put payloads into orbit. Cargo such as propellant and structural materials can be shot into orbit at a much higher acceleration than living things. The Quicklauch Corporation has designed a space gun based upon the work of Canadian engineer Gerald Bull. The Quicklaunch gun would be mounted on a floating platform and be over four hundred meters long, situated in a deep freshwater lake, manmade or natural, near the equator. It would have an initial cost of about a hundred million dollars, which is quite inexpensive for a system to put cargo into orbit.

The gun would use hydrogen compressed to a high pressure, then heated using natural gas to a high temperature increasing the pressure a further five hundred fold. It is then released into the barrel, pushing the projectile out of the muzzle. As the projectile speeds away, the muzzle closes preventing the escape of most of the hydrogen. The vehicle will also have a small rocket engine to push it into orbit and maneuvering rockets to allow docking with another spacecraft or depot. Once the cargo is delivered, the empty shell would be used as building materials in orbit.

Space tethers that would hang down from space, particularly from low Earth orbit, are interesting systems. One of my favorites that would make financial sense as traffic into space increased is the momentum exchange tether or Rotovator. It would decrease the cost of travel to and from Earth Orbit considerably and is well within current technology. It is a rotating tether a hundred and fifty kilometers long. At one end, there would be heavy counterweight and at the other there would be a hook or electromagnetic latch. The Rotovator would have its orbital velocity and the tether rotation rate synchronized. The tether tip would move in a cyclonical curve with respect to the center of rotation. When the tip is at the lowest point it can be momentarily stationary with respect to the ground.

As the hook rotates down it will enter the atmosphere at a speed low enough to grab an aero-spacecraft from the stratosphere. The hook would have wings piloted by a human or computer so that it can be flown and guided thru the upper atmosphere to meet a rising aero-spacecraft. The hook would appear to the pilots like it is coming straight down then would go directly up. The pilots would guide the hook and the vehicle so as to meet at the same place, time and speed. The goal would be to make the grab as gentle as possible. It would then accelerate like a whip to orbital speed, carrying the aero-spacecraft with it. Most of the acceleration would occur well above the atmosphere so little turbulence would be encountered. On the Earth, the tether must stay above most of the atmosphere. On bodies such as the Moon or Mars with little or no atmosphere, the Rotovator tether could actually touch the ground.

Vehicles sent into orbit would be accelerated by the tether, that is, they would gain energy from the tether. Solar panels at the hub would be used to run current down the tether to control the orbital speed and altitude in the Earth's magnetic field. It would also dampen out any vibration. Vehicles returning to the Earth would be attached to the hook in orbit and be slowed down to atmospheric speed. The energy removed from the vehicle would be stored in the rotation for the next grab and acceleration to orbit. It would almost be a free ride up and down with the energy being conserved. In addition, there would be a nice roomy space station at the center of rotation.

Because of the weight, the construction of the Rotovator would be done with materials from the Moon that would be launched into Earth orbit at much less cost than bringing them up from the Earth. The Orion type atomic rocket or space gun could also be utilized to lift the system into orbit. It would be built to last and the cost amortized over a century or more.

The tether could be made of woven Kevlar or something even stronger to reduce weight such as carbon or boron nitride nanotubes, the strongest substances that we are aware of. It would be larger at the hub and tapering toward the hook at the tip. The cost of moving payloads into orbit, either human or cargo, would be about twenty dollars per kilogram, in the range of intercontinental air fare. The cost per kilogram could go even lower as the volume of traffic increased.

Another concept is that it is more efficient to leave the energy supply on the ground so that the weight of the fuel does not have to be lifted. There is a design for a tram into space that would also use a magnetic acceleration like the Chimborazo launcher but would provide the majority of the thrust into orbit. It would be high volume and low cost per launch. It would use a fifteen hundred kilometer long vacuum tunnel and a maglev track. The vehicle would be accelerated using magnetic fields at three times gravity for about five minutes, which would not be a problem for cargo or healthy humans. Most of the track would be on the surface of the Earth but the last fifty kilometers must gently rise out of the atmosphere to a height of about twenty kilometers. The tube itself would be magnetically levitated and use Kevlar or Carbon fiber tethers to hold it in place. The vehicle would emerge at almost orbital velocity. It would then fire a small rocket to overcome any remaining air resistance. It would cost about sixty billion dollars to build, which is a fraction of the cost of the space shuttle, but will be less than fifty dollars per kilogram to Earth orbit.

On the Moon magnetic launches would be much easier because of the lower gravity, lack of an atmosphere and the availability of large amounts of solar generated electricity. The track would be much shorter, only about three hundred kilometers. Launches from the Moon would be nearly horizontal instead of vertical like the Earth because there is no air resistance. Vehicles could be directly launched with enough velocity to take them to the Earth; or once in lunar orbit it could use solar powered thrusters to anywhere else.

Another method that leaves the energy system on the ground and shows a great deal of promise is microwave or laser beam propulsion. The Japanese Space Agency and the U.S. Army have done research and even successfully launched experimental models. There would be an array of low cost microwave transmitters aimed at the vehicle. The high energy beam would heat the air inside of a chamber to a high temperature, the air inside would expand explosively and push the rocket forward with no fuel on board at all. The beam would pulse on and off allowing air to refill the chamber and the process would repeat. Of course, this method would work in the atmosphere but in the upper atmosphere or space it would also have reaction material such as highly compressed hydrogen on board.

In another version, a constant beam would be aimed at heat exchanger on the body of the spacecraft that would transfer heat to the propellant. The propellant is not being burned or oxidized; it is simply being expelled at a constant high velocity. This type of launch system would be much safer than rockets that have been used in the past because it would not carry explosive chemicals. It could carry the payload directly into space without multiple stages dropping off as they are spent. A chemical rocket can have a payload of only about three percent of the total launch weight. The microwave beam rocket could have a payload that is fifteen percent of the launch weight and higher. The microwave transmitters supplying the energy can be powered by any system that can generate electricity and especially clean efficient Thorium power. When solar power stations are built they could provide power for launch or take over providing energy as the vehicle lifted above the stratosphere.

A high volume low cost system is the Lofstrom Loop / Knapman Space Cable. It is a magnetically levitated cable that would cost about ten billion dollars. It is a loop about two thousand kilometers long that would be built in the ocean on the equator with half on the water and the other half eighty kilometers in altitude. It would remain attached to the Earth along its entire length and could be made of Kevlar or carbon nanotubes. It would use linear induction motors to launch vehicles into space and be powered by low cost atomic reactors. In a high volume scenario, perhaps six million tons per year, and an amortization of five years launch costs could be as low as three dollars per kilogram.

One more system that needs to be mentioned, that could eventually be an inexpensive way into orbit, is an elevator. It would be a much more ambitious project and would have far more mass and initial cost than other systems mentioned. It would be a thirty five thousand kilometer long ribbon tethered to the Earth and a counterweight beyond geosynchronous orbit. The counter weight would be moving at more than geosynchronous speed so that it would pull on or put tension on the ribbon. It would not be like a tower but more like a cable holding up a suspension bridge, a really, really long cable.

There would be climber vehicles that would have rollers gripping the ribbon as they ascend, taking about five days to reach the geosynchronous point. If an object, say a brick, is dropped over the side of the climber before it reaches geosynchronous it will fall back to the Earth, if released above it will fly off into space. Only when the payload has reached the geosynchronous point can it be released and will stay in orbit. The climber would obtain energy either from space or the Earth as a microwave or laser beam.

The biggest problem involved is not building the ribbon; it could be lowered from space at the same time extended to the counter-weight from a factory in orbit, chains of fibers being woven together. It could start out as a thin rope and enlarged as it is being built; supplies would be lifted up the ribbon as became larger and stronger. The biggest problem is building the counterweight and keeping it in the right place with the correct tension. It would need a propulsion system to keep it in position. It can be a small captured asteroid with mass added from the Moon or brought up from the Earth. It would be an engineering feat unlike any other but would make the way to space inexpensive and accessible to anyone.

Initially, a viable colony on the Moon could be done for about the same cost as building an aircraft carrier and about as much to maintain. Using this scenario, the amount of equipment would be like putting twenty of the original Apollo lunar landers on Moon; enough to start power generation and life support systems plus a capability to extract raw materials. It could all be done with unmanned cargo shipment before the first payload of humans arrives. The cost would be a mere five percent of the cost of the Space Shuttle program. If the money that was used on the Space Shuttle were instead used to put materials to the Moon, ten thousand tons and twenty people could have been sent to the moon and a self sustaining colony with return to Earth capability could have already been done.

If we invest in the various economical launch systems we can be a true space faring species in short order. Everything that is needed to send people to the Moon and colonize it has already been invented. Most of it has been tested, some of that already in use for many years.

Unfortunately, much of the technology has been socked away in some file cabinet, warehouse or landfill and abandoned. If not for some in powerful positions determined to stop it, the near Earth space environment today would look like what science fiction depicted as what the early 21st century should have been.

Technology

"Technology is a gift of God. After the gift of life it is
perhaps the greatest of God's gifts. It is the mother
of civilizations, of arts and of sciences."

~FREEMAN DYSON

THERE WAS A device in the ancient world called an aeolipile
or Hero's engine that was the first recorded steam turbine. It was
described by Heron of Alexandria in the First Century BC and was
considered a toy. You may have seen pictures of it, a cylindrical vessel on an axle between two posts with angled nozzles coming out of
opposite sides. Water was poured in and then the vessel was heated
until hot steam came out the nozzles. The jet action of the steam
would cause the device to spin quickly until it ran out of water. It
would seem that it would take only a small leap and a few improvements to use the torque created to drive a machine.

It makes one wonder why it took another two thousand years for
steam powered ships to be cruising the Mediterranean. The reason
that the aeolipile did not lead to steam turbines was that human life
and labor was so cheap at that time. The elites, royal families and
their minions knew that all it took was some cheap scraps of food

to keep slaves and serfs going. If there were more laborers needed, simply put some human males and females together and they will happily make more for you. If less were needed, cast them out, murder them or let them starve. Even to this day, technology has not had much of an impact on half of the World's population. Nevertheless, technology has a way of becoming ordinary and ubiquitous and is spreading even into poorest parts of the world.

The best examples of expanding technological access are radio and television. There are few families or communities that do not have access to a radio. Tribes in remote forests of the Amazon, Equatorial Africa or New Guinea will have some form of contact, possibly a television that the entire village watches, powered by a car battery or a small generator. Given all the promise of using radio and television for education, they are mostly used for entertainment and government propaganda. It does educate in some ways; it connects these isolated village people with the rest of the country and even the rest of the world. It maintains their connection with broadcasts in the language of the nation and teaches the young to understand that language.

In native villages in the Amazon, for instance, no matter how isolated, there will always be a few people who can speak Portuguese or Spanish besides their local language. The speed of the dissemination of information is astonishing; for example, the price of precious metals is the same all over the world. You can find many people that are simply unaware of the price, but if you speak to regular traders you will find that they always know the price within an hour or so. If they are in a remote location they will receive the information from the radio and it will be little different than the London or Hong Kong market.

A more recent example is the cellphone. It is surprising that over eighty percent of the world's population has access to cellular telephones. Only about a third has Internet access but that is due more to politics than technology. Cell phones are extraordinary not only as an amazing wireless telephone but for their informational power. Smart phones can access most of the knowledge available to humanity as well as current events, such as it is, being mostly entertainment and sports. It is an invention that allows countries to leap-frog into the future without requiring the much more expensive wired infrastructure. An area the size of a city can have cellphone technology inexpensively installed and it would connect someone who can afford a wireless phone to someone else with such a device anywhere in the world. They are comparatively inexpensive for the user and becoming more so with each passing year. Cellphones can connect people together be they businessmen or lovers.

While communications are necessary for the modern world, some of the most important engineering masterpieces are indoor plumbing, potable water distribution, sanitation systems and sewage treatment. These have had the effects of increasing comfort, reducing disease and prolonging life. The Romans had public baths and toilets, which is the reason their civilization has been emulated for centuries. Roman lavatories were a row of stone seats with a water channel running underneath. The dirty water usually ended up in a river but populations were so low that this pollution was not generally noticeable; and it was "natural". The glory of Rome was due more to its toilets than its armies.

The practical modern toilet was created by a series of inventions in Great Britain in the 1800's. By mid-century most upper class homes had indoor plumbing; it then spread quickly to the rest of the world. The toilet was not invented by Thomas Crapper, as urban legends would have us believe; he improved on the designs and manufactured them. American servicemen in England during World War One saw the name of his company on the eye-height toilet tanks and the slang phrase "going to the Crapper" became common.

Unfortunately, even this level of technology does not affect half of the world's population. The absurdity that many in the poorer half of the world may not have clean water to drink and their toilet is the street, but they will have a cell phone because the infrastructure is so much cheaper to install. Aircraft contrails can be seen in the sky over villages living primarily with Stone Age technology.

Travel and shipping of goods around the world has become commonplace. Summer and winter fruits and vegetables are delivered from the northern and southern hemispheres of the Earth. Seeing tomatoes from Chile in February and cherries from Michigan in the summer is not unusual. There are many examples of technology, seen and unseen. It has allowed humanity to support an ever increasing population and at this time there is still room to grow. Recycling systems would allow ever greater prosperity for more of humanity. Nevertheless, the Earth will eventually run out of easily refined resources; because some of it will escape and be diluted in the ground and oceans. We share the Earth with so many other species and we do not want to cause further damage to the ecosystems during our stewardship of the planet.

There is a picture of the world called "city lights" which was composited from pictures of the Earth from space at night. It shows all of the population centers in the world such as Southeast Asia, India, Europe and Eastern North America. It also shows the vast areas where there are no lights indicating a small or no population. These areas include the huge arctic, desert and jungle areas plus the seventy percent of the planet that are the oceans. The amount of the Earth's surface that is available to humanity to grow food is less than ten percent or about fifty million square kilometers. The rest is about seventy percent salty oceans and the land surface is desert, frozen tundra and mountains.

The easily arable land on the Earth is about the same as the surface area of the Moon but it supports the entire human population and the rest of Earth's creatures are shunted to the less desirable areas. If humans moved to less productive areas then the population could continue to expand with less stress on other creatures and the planet itself. Consider the thirty percent of the planet that is desert;

the primary problem is water. For example, in the US South West, Las Vegas and Phoenix absorb from the entire region. Los Angeles and other cities wring every bit of water that can be found in the Southwest.

Cities are open systems with a massive amount of waste. A more logical way to provide water would be two fold: reclaim wastewater and desalination. Wastewater can be problematic because of all the nasty stuff that people pour down the drain and flush down the toilet. In fact, cities measure drug use by how much metabolized residue there is in the wastewater. It would be much safer to run filtered wastewater thru the same process as desalinated seawater. The solid waste would then be sterilized with chemicals, heated and diluted in set aside wetlands and the result used as fertilizer.

The cost of desalination has been brought down considerably in the last few years. If the energy can be provided by a reliable low cost system, it can make a large volume of potable water from seawater. Where large base power plants are used, instead of using peak power plants, design the base power plant to provide one hundred percent of the power. Then when the power plant is not generating the maximum power at peak times use that energy to desalinate water. Again, if the general wealth can be increased and inexpensive energy made available it would open up even more previously uninhabitable areas.

Using cheap energy from Thorium, anywhere on Earth can become habitable and a comfortable place to live. These new areas include vast desert areas, the arctic and even the Antarctic, which is about as uninhabitable as can be found on the planet Earth. There are designs for huge floating cities and underwater cities. In any of these places, large habitations can be supported using inexpensive energy. Cities could be put in natural and artificial caverns away from inclement weather similar to what would be on the Moon. There is simply not enough solar power at the surface of the Earth to power cities and farms especially those underground without causing even worse damage to the environment but thorium could easily do the trick.

Just as there must be electrical power and data networks; there needs to be stable weather resistant transportation networks. High speed rail systems cover Europe and they should be expanded to cover the planet. Air travel is for people with enough money who want to get somewhere quickly. Rail is a more comfortable way to travel, with the transportation networks in Europe and Japan the model. This project would drive technology as well as world peace. There would need to be a bridges or tunnels across the Gibraltar Strait between Spain and Morocco Africa as well as another across the Bering Strait between Alaska and Siberia. All of the continents except Antarctica would be connected. There would be countless other feats of engineering. There would be millions of people employed around the world to build, maintain this monumental project.

The greatest project for humanity will be to move much of the population off planet Earth where it can grow as it will. There can be rules established where technology is applied on Earth only when it doesn't impact the environment by recycling or using organic substances which break down to simpler compounds with seawater, sunlight or bacteria. These substances include paper and the many types of biodegradable plastics. Perhaps, when most of humanity is living away from the Earth and the population of the planet is much smaller, limits to technology can be established that would minimize impact. There would be trade and the Earth born would maintain relationships with the space born.

As has been shown, the Moon is truly the stepping stone to the colonization of the solar system and the greater universe. The Moon does not have an ecosystem to damage but to create, it can support a population in the billions. Surfaces of planets can be dangerous; it makes little sense to colonize other planets as an alternative to the Earth. The Colonization of other planets to provide raw materials and factories make a great deal of sense.

After the Moon, the most important planet to be colonized is not Mars, but Mercury. It is an ideal source for energy and raw materials. It is close to the sun so there is plentiful solar energy; about nine times more than in Earth orbit. It is also a source for heavy metals that are not easily available elsewhere. It is less than three times the volume of the Moon but is over four times heavier. It can be mined for construction materials and would have underground cities similar to the moon where miners, technicians and their families would live. With about one third of the gravity of the Earth, it would be good place to live. The entire surface area is as big as half the land area of the Earth or Asia and Africa combined. There are habitable areas at the poles, where the day to night temperature is not as extreme that is larger than the entire European Union. The rest of the planet would be mines and launching equipment.

The surface gravity and escape velocity of Mercury are about twice as much as the Moon but still only one third of the earth. Like the Moon, it also has no life forms to consider. Using solar energy, construction and raw materials can be inexpensively launched to a required orbit. Hydrogen would be harvested from the solar wind and combined with oxygen from Mercury to form water. The crust of Mercury being over forty percent oxygen there is a large amount of water available for the local population and export.

There could be mirrors and other solar power collectors in orbit around Mercury that would be used to smelt metal. The mirrors and collectors would beam the energy down to the surface. There could be lakes of molten materials ready to be formed; including iron, steel, aluminum, magnesium and glass. Mercury seems to be even richer in titanium than the Earth's Moon. Construction materials can be cast and formed in the gravity of Mercury then launched to be assembled in orbit.

Sending finished and construction materials into orbit around Mercury would be much less costly compared to the Earth and even to the Moon considering the much larger amount of solar energy available. Solar collectors would be engineered to handle the much higher power density. It would take about ten Kilowatt hours to move one kilogram into Mercury orbit or about one square meter of solar collector. The cost per ton into orbit would be fractions of a dollar.

Venus also has a great deal of potential, but not because of the minerals located on its surface. They would be difficult to reach because of the thick atmosphere, high temperatures and high gravity. The atmosphere of Venus is a treasure trove of carbon, nitrogen, chlorine, fluorine and other elements that are not easily available on Mercury. Automated solar powered ships or tethered balloons would collect the gas. They would be compressed to liquid form to be distributed on orbital trajectories in the near solar system. The oxygen could be sent to the Moon to form a thin atmosphere for micrometer and cosmic ray protection.

What to do with all this power and construction materials? Create even more safe and comfortable places for people to live. Places that would ensure the continued survival of humanity into the future. It appears from the current state of our understanding of the workings of the Universe that the speed of light is indeed the speed limit for material objects. What this means is that the majority of humanity will be contained in our solar system for quite some time. Our Sun will provide energy for billions of years, more than enough time for Earthlife including humanity to evolve into new forms. There is plenty of space, energy and matter around the Sun to provide for our progeny far into the future.

Habitats

Every day is a journey, and the journey itself is home.

~Matsuo Basho

PLANETS CAN NOT be the future home for the majority of mankind. They have high gravity, wild weather and other unpredictable catastrophes. The biggest reason is that they do not have enough habitable area. There is another future that would be the permanent home for humankind, artificial planetoids or habitats. They were elucidated by American physicist Gerard O'Neill. In his book, "The High Frontier: Human Colonies in Space" he preferred a location near the Earth - Moon system, which may a good idea in the short term, but a different location would make more sense for the long term. The best site for habitats would take advantage of the resources of solar energy, manufactured material from Mercury and light elements from Venus. They would be in orbit around Venus and Mercury or in solar orbit between them.

Mercury is a resource for heavy metals, so the habitats could be made from much stronger and inexpensive iron alloys instead of aluminum alloys. Using energy from the Sun, iron could be extracted and formed into high quality steel construction materials. Factories would be located on and in orbit around Mercury. There is plenty of power from the Sun available. Solar collectors would be located on the surface and in mercurial orbit and the power beamed to the surface. There is nothing living to get in the way so the beams can be extremely high energy.

The habitats would be built of steel, concrete and aluminum as the primary construction materials. They will also use long life glass, fiberglass and silicon plastics all of which would be easily fabricated on Mercury. Mirrors in orbit around the planet would be used to smelt and create lakes of molten metal ready to use. The Mercurial workforce would live in comfort in underground cities similar to those on the Moon. It would be more efficient to have some of the factories on the surface of Mercury and have pre-made construction materials sent to up to construction sites in orbit. Were I a later day entrepreneur, I would invest all my money in Mercurial mining and manufacturing.

A design for the habitats would be a cylinder where one of the flat ends would always face the Sun to collect energy. The other end of the cylinder would be used for landing and launching of spacecraft. O'Neill envisioned cylinders to be hollow on the inside with a huge amount of empty space. It had mirrors and windows to light the inside surface of a hollow cylinder. He could not have foreseen low cost, efficient LED lighting technology. His concept would be inefficient and expensive to build. If there were windows and mirrors, there would be more of a problem shielding against high energy particles. It would be more practical to build sealed habitats where there would be living spaces inside like stories in a building or concentric cylinders going toward the center. The levels would have decreasing centrifugal force, as one moved toward the axis, which would feel like decreasing gravity.

A good size for a habitat would be fifteen kilometers in diameter and fifteen kilometers long shaped like a common can of soup. The dimensions of the soup can are the solution to a classic calculus problem, that is, how to maximize the enclosed volume of a cylinder with the minimum surface area. This design would have an external surface area of over seven hundred square kilometers, about the same size as the nation of Singapore. It is truly a world on its own.

The axis of rotation would be the center line thru the two flat ends. Rotation would create artificial gravity by centrifugal force for the comfort of the inhabitants. The floor would be outward toward the circumference away from the axis. The speed of rotation would be adjusted to somewhere between Earth and lunar gravity. By this time there would have been many generations born on the Moon and medical problems caused by living in low gravity would have been solved.

Earth-like gravity at the circumference would be made by one rotation every three minutes. Lunar type gravity would created by one rotation every seven minutes. Perhaps something in between, about the same as Mars or Mercury would work out the best. A lower speed of rotation would put less stress on the structure so that it could be built for less cost. The habitat is so large and the rotation slow enough it would not be felt by the inhabitants. The "gravity" would decrease as one moved toward the axis of rotation. There would be counter-rotating mechanisms at the axis to keep such things as antennas and cameras stable.

There could be fifty platforms or levels, each one hundred meters tall, built concentrically from the outside toward the center. There would be an internal living space of over twenty thousand square kilometers that is about thirty times the size of Singapore. The habitat would be built like a suspension bridge, with cables from the central core, each cable balanced by another going the opposite direction. The external shell and the platforms various internal levels would be suspended from the cables. The structure would certainly be strong enough and it is not a new technology. The Brooklyn Bridge was finished in 1883. A group of suspension bridges were built in Bhutan in 1433, constructed with iron chain; the last one washed away in

2004. The longest and largest bridges in the world are all suspension bridges.

The interior would be sealed from the vacuum of space to prevent air leakage. Construction would be done with interlocking plates as large as two kilometers square held together with cables and bands made of high tensile strength materials. It would be sealed with long lasting, inexpensive silicone plastics. The habitat would be compartmentalized to minimize air and water leakage until repairs could be made. Maximum safety would be assured by an inner and outer exterior wall. There could a layer of ice in between which would make a good particle shield as well as insulation. It would also be a reserve of water, oxygen and hydrogen and anything else that could be dissolved in the water. Weight would not be that much of an issue because of the low cost of launches from Mercury. There are enough raw materials on Mercury to make billions such habitats.

There would be solar panels and tethers to collect energy from sunlight and the solar wind that would be converted to electricity. It would be used to power lights, pumps, data systems and everything else. It would also be used to create a magnetic field to deflect high energy particles. There would be electric cannons or launchers to defect and prevent larger objects from striking the habitat. Air conditioning and heating would not be large consumers of power because the temperature of the habitat would be regulated. There would also be exterior radiators to remove excess heat.

The habitat would also rotate very slowly perpendicular to its axis, about once every 150 days, to keep one end of the cylinder always pointed at the Sun. This end would be the solar energy collector as well as the radiation and solar particle shield. Electrical power generated would be about four times the size of the average city sized power plant on Earth. It will be a resource of more than twenty Gigawatt hours of power per day, certainly more than enough to power whatever is needed. Power and heat intake can be regulated by placing movable mirrors on the Sun side to allow unneeded sunlight to pass beyond to the habitat. An orbit between Mercury and Venus would provide four times as much solar power as reaches the Earth – Moon system. This side would have the most shielding against high energy particles from the Sun. If the habitat were to be located farther from the Sun, for example in Earth or Mars orbit, mirrors could be used to direct more sunlight into the collector.

The other end of the cylinder away from the Sun would be used for transportation between habitats and the launching and receiving freight. The rotation of the cylinder would be used to launch spacecraft on calculated trajectories. This process would reduce the angular momentum of the habitat but returning spacecraft would be slowed down. Its energy would be returned to the rotation of the habitat and reused for the next launch. The habitat itself would be used to store this energy.

Spacecraft would speed down extended arms to magnify the velocity and the launch would be timed correctly so that its trajectory would intersect its target. Since they will not be landing on planets, the inter-habitat spacecraft would be simple units that would use inertia and electric propulsion powered by the Sun. The habitat itself would use electric propulsion for station keeping, to maintain the correct rotation and the correct orbital position with respect to the Sun and other habitats.

The inner surface of the outermost level, the farthest from the axis of rotation, could be the area of lakes and water sports. It would make sense, because any internal water flow would be to this level. It would also be one of the areas for water storage and heat regulation. There could be drains from the inner levels that would end up in this little world ocean where it could be filtered and recycled. There would be plumbing that would distribute filtered and cleaned water and air at the axis to be recycled to every part of the structure. Circulating water would also be used for heating and cooling

There would be sprinkler systems for artificial rain and firefighting as well as agriculture. As on the Earth and lunar settlements, forests for wood could be grown to provide interior construction materials as well as atmospheric cleansing and beauty. There is plenty of room for farms that would supplement the hydroponic gardens. There would be parks as well as "wild" areas that could have selected plants and animals from the Earth, as well as some genetically engineered ones.

In the hundred meter tall open areas, looking toward the circumference, it would be over a kilometer to the little world's horizon. Looking toward the circumference, it would be like looking uphill. The ceilings of each level could be painted or better, they could be covered in LED's to make a giant television type display, like Freemont Street in Las Vegas. The display could be whatever the citizens wanted, even changed on schedule. It could display cameras from outside so that the interior would seem transparent without the rotation. The display could also make it seem like the interior were far larger, even a planetary surface. It could give the inhabitants the feeling of mountains, valleys, sunsets and sunlit summer days.

The farthest one could be from the lake level would be a seven and a half kilometer elevator ride to the axis. There would be horizontal and vertical transportation corridors that would move people and materials around the world. They could be powered either by electricity or air pressure as in a pneumatic tube. Again, energy would be conserved by capturing it as materials moved away from the axis and reused for materials moving toward the axis.

Each level could be one hundred meters tall and stacked inward to where the "gravity" is one third of the bottom floor. There would then be about fifty primary living levels each with an average surface area of Los Angles or about five hundred square kilometers. Our habitat would have a total livable surface area larger than Israel or the American State of New Jersey. There could be levels with apartment blocks and others with park areas and soil, ponds, streams with meadows and trees. It would make sense that living and sleeping areas would be where the gravity would be the most comfortable inner levels. It would also be where cosmic ray penetration would be negligible.

The habitat could comfortably support a population with the density of Singapore, which would have a total population of over a hundred million. Perhaps, that should be considered the maximum size. A population the same as the Netherlands or sixteen million would seem to be a good size with lots of open areas set aside. There could be apartment blocks and even stand alone homes and with parks and trees. It would seem to be a convenient nation size.

If there were many habitats with an interactive well educated, politically active population would be the best way to sustain humanity. Each habitat could be diverse with different populations and ecologies. They could be colonized by different cultures from Earth. There could be the Anglo, Chinese, Spanish, Russian, Arabic, Japanese or whatever. All types of civilizations and governments are possible. Keeping with the wishes of the citizens, each habitat could go their own way in culture and politics. The interior would be built out as population expanded to be paid for by the new comers either as children of the original population or as immigrants.

There would be loose confederations of worlds that would collaborate on projects such as biotechnology, antimatter production, spacecraft and habitat manufacturing. Some of the habitats could specialize in manufacturing, others in farming and others to create fuel for round trips to Earth and the inner planets as well as the outer solar system. There would be a great deal of trade and there could be every type of human society and much that we can't conceive of at this point in time.

There would need to be political mechanisms so that monopolization of access to resources does not happen. Since we are human, the concept of powerful families will probably not go away. The Rockefellers did not become wealthy from oil wells but by controlling the distribution systems. Since all the worlds would recycle to a great degree, armed conflicts would be expensive and unimaginably dangerous. Conquest of "new" territory would be ridiculous; it would be far cheaper to build new habitats.

The habitat would certainly be roomy enough and that is not including the inner two and a half kilometers from the center of reduced "gravity" and weightlessness. This area would have a volume of almost three hundred cubic kilometers. That is where the factories, hydroponic farms, recycling and repair facilities could be located as well as reservoirs of raw materials. Perhaps, one of the levels could be filled with salt water to create a world ocean and for the production of Earth-type seafood.

As in all spacecraft, the habitat would recycle resources, but there would be plenty of inexpensive energy available and the costs of reuse would be minimal. If there were some loss of water or air, perhaps caused by an undetected meteor, the leak would be plugged and repairs made as is done by maintenance crews as in any city. The habitats would be resupplied with air, water or any anything else with materials easily available in the Solar System.

The cost of a habitat per ton would be inexpensive because it will be built like a suspension bridge that is mostly mass and would not be built to survive the weather on Earth. The stress points will not be changing. The habitats would be built with the same standard modular design so the cost could be kept down. The interior levels could be added as the population expanded to minimize initial construction costs.

We can guess that the habitat would cost about sixteen quadrillion in 2010 dollars to build. We can also hope that the wealth of mankind would have greatly increased. Consider the fact that the average American, European, Chinese or Japanese do things as normal routine daily activities that would be the stuff of fantasy of his ancestors. The cost of construction could be spread over the sixteen million inhabitants but it could also be amortized, at low interest for hundreds of years or even over several lifespans. If the lifespan of the average person were extended to be over a thousand years it would be a trifle.

This beautiful concept will be economically feasible when there is a large space born population long independent from Earth resources. It is an indicator of what is possible even with present day technology. If there is a population on Earth stabilized at about twenty billions and a Lunar population of another twenty billion and a few million more on Mercury plus some on small scale space habitats; it would make sense to begin building large space habitats that would become a very long term home for humanity. The construction of habitats may be five hundred or a thousand years from now but it is certainly a lovely future.

Flourish

We humans are an extremely important manifesta-
tion of the replication bomb, because it is through
us - through our brains, our symbolic culture and our
technology - that the explosion may proceed to the
next stage and reverberate through deep space.

~RICHARD DAWKINS

FOR THE FIRST few thousands of years into the age of space
habitats they would most likely be located in the same orbital plane
as the planets for ease of travel. Transportation from one habitat to
another or to a planet would be a simple low energy orbit. They would
mostly be located between Venus and Mercury for solar energy and,
again, for ease of travel. Habitats with similar cultures and interests
would cluster together. There would be rings of orbits from seventy
to ninety million kilometers from the Sun.

If the habitats were a thousand kilometers from each other, there
could be over a billion habitats spaced like pearls on a necklace on the
various orbits. The gravity of the Sun would dominate so there will be
little perturbation by other habitats or even planets. If they all had
an average population of sixteen million, the total human population

would be eight trillion or a thousand times the current population of the Earth. For all its immensity, it still would not still look like the ring around Saturn. Habitats would only be visible from the Earth with a powerful telescope.

There is a concept called megascale engineering, that is, structures larger than a million meters or a thousand kilometers. There are a few examples on the Earth, the oldest being the Great Wall of China. There are also the rail and highway systems, engineered rivers, containerized cargo and the Internet. There are concepts for far larger systems. Freeman Dyson, physicist and mathematician, had a thought experiment that lead to the concept of a shell around the Sun. This shell, called a Dyson Sphere, could eventually make use of a large part of the power of the sun. It could not be a hard surface; the engineering of such a thing is many, many years in the future, if even possible.

The habitats in various orbits around the Sun between Mercury and Venus would form a shell like bees buzzing around the hive. They would take advantage of solar power but be far enough for safety from the sun and at a safe distance from one another. If the space between Mercury and Venus were considered, it would have volume of two with twenty-four zeros behind it (in scientific notation), cubic kilometers. Each habitat could be allocated a torus or a doughnut shape of a trillion cubic kilometers with the Sun in the center.

The shell between Mercury and Venus would allow about two billion habitats with a total population well over a million billion inhabitants. That is over a million times the current population of the Earth. Combined, they would provide a habitable area a million times the land area of the Earth. Nevertheless, if the shell were full of habitats as described, it would block less than one millionth of the energy from the Sun. There is no new science needed, again, all that has been described can be done current science and some creative engineering.

Space born populations in the millions of billions would make the terraforming of planets seem like a waste of time unless some folks want to do it as a hobby but they could still be used for raw materials. The Earth would be a museum and a tourist destination, much of it could return to the "wild" state, with large areas becoming parks. There may be humans still living on the planet but they would be in a much lower concentration. Space born human tourists may not want to, or be able to visit the surface of the Earth because of the high gravity. They would still visit with robotic sensors.

Besides the habitats, there will be underground human cities on most of the moons of the Solar System and the inner planets. The exception would be Venus, where there would be cloud cities like the fictional planet of Bespin in the "Star Wars" movie. They would harvest important elements from the thick soupy atmosphere, such as carbon, nitrogen, sulfur, argon and Xenon. It is another advantage of our solar system, heavy elements from Mercury and light elements from Venus conveniently nearby. Space ships would land on other planets, including the Earth, Mercury and Mars, with enough anti-matter fuel to return to space.

There could be habitats in orbit around the outer planets that would collect energy from the gas giant planets or have giant mirrors that would collect as much solar energy as habitats closer into the Sun. The moons of the outer planets could also be inhabited. There could be cities built in the one hundred kilometer thick surface ice of Europa if no life is found there. The truth of a better life for the trillions of unborn humans is space habitats. The award winning science fiction author, Larry Niven, once said "Building a space station for everyone is insane: we should have built a dozen." I say we need to build millions and billions.

The habitats described are actually spacecraft and have station keeping propulsion systems that could also be used to move it around the Solar System. It is a good bet that some people on some of the habitats would wish to travel to other stars. If it became so crowed that living with trillions of other humans within trillions of cubic kilometers became intolerable they could move to a more spacious neighborhood. There is plenty of room on the habitat for a more powerful propulsion system to be added. Additional engines, fuel and shielding could be attached to the habitat either mechanically, tethered or magnetically.

They could take years spiraling to orbits farther and farther from the Sun increasing speed day by day, year by year to accelerate to a fraction of light speed. We can calculate that a habitat with an acceleration of one thousandth of Earth gravity that would eventually reach a maximum velocity of five percent of the speed of light during a trip to the nearest stars, the Alpha Centari system. This acceleration would be so gentle so that "down" would still be the same direction from the axis toward the outermost levels. It would take about a hundred years to reach the nearest star system, including acceleration away from the Sun and decelerating at the other end of the journey.

For even longer trips, a device called a Bussard interstellar ramjet would be used. It would collect hydrogen and helium atoms between the stars with a magnetic field like a gigantic net thousands of kilometers across. They would use a nuclear fusion process for propulsion. For those living on board, there would be little concern by the inhabitants while moving, because the systems would be robust and life would go on as normal.

Since they are self-contained worlds with total recycling, there is no need for habitable planets at the other end of a journey, only sources for raw materials such as asteroids and solar wind. They can also use giant mirrors and solar collectors, hydrogen fusion, and even antimatter for power, all of which will be available at the local star. The people on the habitat around the new star would have access to all human knowledge and they would still be in communication with the rest of humanity. They could start up other factories around the new star to produce more habitats. This could continue indefinitely.

At one tenth of the speed of light there are a dozen stars within a hundred years of travel. There are over ten thousand in a thousand year journey and over a million within ten thousand years. Given a million years, again at one tenth light speed, the entire galaxy could be colonized. Since all intelligent inhabitants would be genetically related, it would be the realm of Isaac Asimov or Gene Roddenberry's Star Trek. Captain Kirk would actually be able to make whoopee with space women.

Perhaps we should consider if there are other intelligent species that could have accomplished the same thing. We have an ongoing search for extraterrestrials called the Search for Extraterrestrial Intelligence or SETI. A great deal of time, effort and money is spent on SETI. If they exist, communications with space aliens may be possible but unlikely. If we were astronomically lucky (or unlucky) and our potential communicants evolved nearby, we would need to have roughly the same level of intelligence and technology. If they were just a little bit less intelligent, perhaps, they would still be living in their equivalent of trees. If they were more intelligent than us, would they want to communicate with us? How detailed are your communications with your dog or cat, which are relatively intelligent critters? How about a cockroach?

Assuming that the time and the direction were correct, the window of technology is tiny, a hundred years or less. In a mere hundred years, we humans have already technologically passed beyond simple analog radio transmissions. The majority of the signals emanating from Earth at this point in time are low power compressed digital information almost indistinguishable from noise. All that said, SETI is a marvelous way to fund astronomical research, and that is always desirable. Interestingly, nothing that would indicate intelligence has been found so far.

Travel and communication between the stars is challenging because of the distances but perhaps space aliens are now colonizing the galaxy or altruistically just flying around looking for "friends".

There is a problem with that too; pushing matter at a speed great enough to travel between stars requires a lot of energy. An interstellar spacecraft anywhere near the Earth would have already been seen because of the prodigious amounts needed. If they were coming toward the Earth, the energy and light would be hugely blue shifted, making it obvious. The habitat at maximum velocity during our hypothetical trip to the nearest star would have as much energy as the entire Earth receives from the Sun in a day.

Space aliens in science fiction books and movies have been portrayed as either monsters or as saviors of humanity. Monsters would be most improbable. Why use astronomical amounts of energy just to get a meal? One would think that any sufficiently intelligent beings who could engineer spacecraft could also build places to live with some decent restaurants. Raw materials are the same everywhere and abundant in the Universe so there is no conflict to be found there. Saviors from our own "evils" are just as unlikely.

If they do exist, space is very large and as shown in the numbers above, there is plenty of room to expand. There is a potential for trillions of inhabitants around a single star and there are billions of stars in the galaxy. Personally, I would look forward to another species, terrestrial or extraterrestrial, to share and explore the Universe with. Nevertheless, why should it not be humanity that colonizes the galaxy? The Fermi-Hart paradox asks the question: if extraterrestrial intelligent life is common where are they? Where is the evidence of their existence? The Rare Earth hypothesis goes on to say that life may be common but only, at best, as single cell organisms. As mentioned, humanity could spread throughout the galaxy in a million years. If there were space faring cultures that preceded us, they would already be here.

There are intelligent creatures living among us right here on Earth. There could even be habitats of tool using cetaceans (dolphins and orcas), parrots, corvids (crows and ravens), elephants and even octopi. Humans adapted for water or wings could join them. They could also create environments that have not been thought of at this point in time.

As the years pass in the hundreds of thousands, human evolution and technology will go where we can't imagine. Stars are sources of energy so it would make sense that humanity would gravitate to them. It would be possible to have habitats in between stars or even between galaxies using large energy collection mirrors. They would be lonely outposts, but the view of a nearby galaxy filling half the sky with without obscuring cosmic dust would be breathtaking.

A yellow star similar to our Sun will have a lifetime of about ten billion years but they account for only about seven percent of the stars in the galaxy. An orange or red star with less than half the mass of the Sun will have a lifetime of fifty billion years, ten times that of our Sun. They constitute ninety percent of the stars in the Universe. The habitable zone of an orange red dwarf star is much smaller so that a planet or habitat would need to be much closer in to the star. Instead of the eighty five million kilometers for an orbit around our Sun, it would be more like eight million. Our sun appears to us as the size of a quarter held at arm's length. An orange-red dwarf star at a distance that would provide the same energy would appear five to ten times bigger or about the size of a basketball held arm's length.

The planets of such a dwarf star would be tidally locked with one side constantly facing the star much as the Moon shows only one face to the Earth. One side would be ever hotter and the other ever cooler and any atmosphere would freeze out on the dark side. This would not be a problem for space habitats because they are designed to have one face to the star anyway. Data collected from the Kepler telescope indicates that comets, asteroids and, to a lesser degree, planets are common and could be used for resources.

At our point in time all of humanity is in one place, one planet. If we destroy our planet by warfare, overpopulation or ecological damage we may lose the ability to move off planet. Anything can happen; a massive volcano or the impact of an asteroid from space can return the Earth to an ice age. The Earth is impacted by rocks from space, meteors, every second of every day. Most are too small to do anything other than become a streak of light burning up with friction thru the atmosphere. There are larger meteors that make it to the surface of the Earth, mostly in the oceans. There are also mountain-sized rocks that could extinguish all life on Earth.

Damaging the ability to move off the planet does not have to be an extinction event. There are many dangers on and off the Earth that could destroy civilization. Another is a giant solar flare, which are massive outbursts of electrified particles from our own Sun. There is a possibility of a nearby star exploding into a supernova. A virulent disease could jump from another species or be weaponized and kill the majority of people. There are reckless and greedy oligarchs tearing down science and engineering for short-term gain. They increase the possibility of wars and the possibility of humanity destroying itself.

When humans are living on the Moon and habitats in the thousands and millions, even a Jupiter sized disturbance could destroy only a small fraction of humanity. We have the ability to move, at least, a few humans and our companion species off the planet Earth to a safer place. We must take advantage of the technology that we have. It will be the greatest thing that has ever happened and will employ billions of people for thousands and thousands of years to come.

Given advances in technology, the life spans of humans would be far greater than now. We could alter our environments to suit ourselves we could also alter ourselves for life in any sort of environment. We can make environments that we are most comfortable. Most of the stories in science fiction that include travel between worlds would work out the same with travel between habitats. The technology, adventure and stories will be beyond today's science fiction. When the habitats begin to travel to other stars is when the human experience becomes transcendent.

Humanity

Sometimes it falls upon a generation to be great, you can be that generation.

~NELSON MANDELA

THERE ARE THINGS that Homo sapiens can do that other creatures can not... besides browse the Internet. Extreme evolutionary stress on humanity has given us advantages over not only other creatures but also other human species that have existed. One of these special human abilities can be seen at a baseball game. There are no other animals that can throw as fast or as accurately as humans. There are stories of chimpanzees throwing feces at zoo visitors. Perhaps they do it to shoo them away, but to be hit one would have to be quite unlucky. A human at a distance of a few yards would not miss. We seem to have an innate ability to judge trajectories and air resistance of thrown objects such as rocks.

Language defines humanity; there are no other creatures that can communicate such complex concepts and cooperate far beyond any others. It is one of the primary uses of our large brains. It is not known whether it is one of the stimuli to develop a large brain or is a result of having one. Language allows humans to draw on the knowledge of their ancestors and with the invention of writing, all of history.

Because of language, complex culture and knowledge passes from generation to generation. It is used to define differences between groups of people. Human culture is a tapestry of history, language, technology, religion and tradition. Spoken language is the crowning achievement of human evolution and written language is the crowning achievement of human invention. The capability of learning and understanding written symbols is what set humanity on the path to technology and the way to the stars.

Before the invention of writing and libraries, the elderly of the tribe were repositories of information and there is a good reason this is true. Humans live much longer than our evolutionary cousins, the great apes or other similar sized creatures. We live nearly three times longer than chimpanzees. This gift allows humanity a longer time to learn and teach younger generations and transmit survival information across generations. It appears that humans have a better immune as well as other systems that repair damage better than most other mammals. This ability seems to have developed as a result of being the most carnivorous of the great apes.

No other species has the ability to control fire. Fearing it, they get as far away as they can. Fire is how early humans kept predators at bay and was one of the tools besides the hammer and sharp edge that early humans learned how to use. Evidence of fire usage has been found at human archeological sites as old as a quarter of a million years. The use of fire for light and heat would give a tribe a huge advantage over neighbors.

Fire allowed another early invention that changed the evolution of humanity, the cooking of food. Cooking is an important skill indeed. Most foods are tough and difficult to chew, cooking softens food, kills bacteria and adds flavor. Cooking foods allowed for smaller teeth and jaw muscles and paved the way for complex speech. When some ancient genius discovered the smelting of metal by heat and fire, it greatly advanced the ability to make and use tools and weapons. They were used against prey animals and other humans.

The ability to make use of objects outside of our bodies, tools and weapons, to enhance our survivability is extremely well developed in humans. Other species are adept at using tools such as rocks and sticks. There are many examples: monkeys use rocks to crack nuts, chimpanzees use a carefully selected twig to harvest termites and some birds use a twig to probe for insects. Monkeys in Japan have learned to use seawater to clean sand and mud from potatoes and rice and add flavor. Humans use everything from sticks to super-computers.

The hunting and gathering way of living limited the expansion of humanity. Because of the difficulty of extracting food from the environment thru the year, the size of communities was limited. The tribe generally had to be mobile to follow herds and the life cycle of plants. The human ability to plan for the future and being able to predict the consequences of ones actions enabled the invention of agriculture. Control over the environment facilitated the harvest and storage of food thru lean months. Cultivation of grains and the husbandry of goats, sheep, dogs, pigs and cattle became common as each generation passed on the knowledge.

Agriculture made domination of an area easier because of larger populations. Nearby tribes that still survived using the hunter-gatherer lifestyle were driven away or exterminated. Farming facilitated the exponential growth of human populations. It had the advantage of freeing up some of the individuals in the tribe to specialize and develop technologies such as botany, medicine, constructing living spaces and making tools and weapons. Occupations such as breeding plants and animals, manufacturing and, of course, soldiering developed to expand control over their environment. It was agriculture that enabled humanity to become the dominant large animal on the planet. What followed was the building of huge cities, nations and continent wide empires. It is also what will allow the colonization of the Moon and solar system.

Humans have the ability to live in small tribes much as the other great apes do but also in huge confusing cities with an overwhelming amount of stimuli. It is done by narrowing ones interactive group; everyone has their own tribe or clique within the larger whole. Humans reduce aggression in crowds by looking upon other humans as part of the environment such as trees or harmless herd animals. If they did not, and some cannot, the stress would be unbearable. Human brutality is controlled and relatively rare unless industrialized by government as in war. Huge conglomerations of humans live together in cities and they are generally peaceful places with a great deal of entertainment. In fact, if properly governed and maintained, cities can be idyllic places to live.

One of the greatest abilities of humanity that is not found on any list is the ability to entertain one another. Creatures will generally watch what others in their group are doing. They need to be aware of any possible danger and if there is any food over there. They need to pay attention to dominance displays or get a good thumping. Humans have a unique capacity to be amused not only by each other but by "humanizing" animals or even natural events. It requires many traits to come together such as empathy, cooperation, a redirected flight response and the fact that we enjoy each other's company. Humans can listen to story tellers and imagine themselves in the story. It can be comedy, acting, singing, music and religion. Religion is indeed a form of entertainment that can take place as regularly as once a week. It was generally forbidden to work on the day of worship, which is probably one of the reasons it became so popular. Festivals are common with all religions.

Thomas Malthus wrote in the late Eighteenth century that food production would grow much slower than population, always leading to starvation of some. The reason (for the mathematically inclined) is that production can only increase linearly but population will grow exponentially. It applies to all creatures including humans. Humans can seem to be cruel to one another, people are allowed to suffer and die if others see a greater good. That "good" can be the greed of the elites or the belief that "our" group is more important than another group. Generally, it was not deliberate cruelty but the viewpoint that it is a natural law and nothing can be done to change it.

Human starvation has been common thru all of history but not completely due to the Malthusian process. As examples, the Irish famine that drove so many to the Americas was more than the potato blight but also the English landowners maximizing their profits. Potatoes were exported while the Irish population was starving. The Soviets under Stalin exported wheat instead of feeding the people, which caused as many as ten million Ukrainians to die of starvation. Forty million Chinese starved during the political upheavals of Mao's "Great Leap Forward". In the mid-Twentieth Century, starvation was common around the world, Africa, across Asia from the Middle East to the Far East and China due to poor government, war and overpopulation compared to the food supply.

There is a hero in this: Norman Borlaug, the father of the "Green Revolution". He was an American scientist who did research in Mexico to create high yield varieties of wheat. He was able to change the conundrum of population growing faster than the food supply. Mexico went from starvation to become an exporter of wheat and corn. The high yield plants were then planted in India and Pakistan, which more than doubled their food supply. In 1963, India was able to increase their crop and went from about a ton of wheat per hectare to seven tons per hectare. The Chinese also started using high yield rice and adapted to his techniques and achieved similar results. There were many skeptics who said that starvation was inevitable that he proved wrong. Not only were people eating better but living healthier, having more time for education and to improve their lives.

The best way to stabilize human population is not genocide but female education, simply because women control the birth rate. It is an unfortunate truism that affluent, more educated women will have fewer children. Those in poverty or poorly educated tend to be more prolific. Population control happens as a society becomes more prosperous. The driving force appears to be societal acceptance of female education and intelligence. In every educated country in the world there has been a dramatic drop in the birthrate. Many countries have a negative birthrate and are even reducing their population. In most of Europe, China, Japan and Russia there has been reduction in the birth rate and the population. The countries with the lowest birth rates are Catholic Spain and traditionalist Japan.

It is a fact that the most intelligent among us rise to the top to be in positions of control. They are the cognitive elites, the top end of the statistical Bell curve of brainpower. They are generally the ones that are responsible for recent history and current events, the movers and shakers of the world. This group generally controls the lives of the rest of humanity. Not all gifted people go into positions of leadership, many have other interests, but in general they will have a propensity for leadership positions. Wise leaders will use them to help make decisions.

The cognitive elites in the United States are schooled in the so-called Ivy League universities and are in control of academia, corporate offices and government. It is a similar situation in all parts of the world. Most of them have been indoctrinated in the philosophy of the progressivism that has its roots in the labor struggles in the late Nineteenth and early Twentieth Centuries. It is now little more than a catchword for fascistic big government social engineering and destructive high taxes. There is no question that the cognitive elites are in control but whether they make good decisions for the benefit of all humanity is another question.

If the Cognitive elite of about ten percent of humanity is controlling the fate of humanity what are the other ninety percent doing? They are much more than the experimental animals of the elites; they are the fulcrum that the elites stand upon. They are the wellspring of humanity, where all of us come from. They, if allowed, will provide for themselves and will do fine governing themselves by creating their own cognitive elites as has been done since the first human families and tribes. They really don't need the existing elites; they will create their own.

There are millions of peasants in China, India, Africa and many other places in the world that survive in what we, in the industrial-ized world, would consider wrenching poverty. They would consider their lives comfortable with enough food to eat, a place to sleep and family to care for each other. There is little conflict and if there is, it is handled locally by the communities themselves. Occasionally they will produce a genius that can change everything.

The most important group of humanity is those people that can be called the vanguard or change makers. Change is a well worn slogan for politicians but these individuals are the ones, for good or evil, which truly pulls humanity into the future, another paradigm. Some come from elites but many more come from greater human-ity. They are the people that truly cause real change thru their own efforts and actions. They may be lucky, being at the right place at the right time. They come from all backgrounds and are the vision-aries, inventors, the social activists. Their activities may be slight or profound, deliberate or accidental. They may not even be aware of their importance to humanity. Historically, some are known by their own names but others accomplishments went by the name of a cause or other notoriety.

A few examples of people that have made the great changes in the world are religious leaders like Mohamed, Siddhartha Gautama (Buddha) and Saul of Tarsus (Apostle Paul). There have been mili-tary leaders like Genghis Khan, Alexander, Qin Shi Huang, and Charlemagne; scientists and inventors like Isaac Newton, James Watt, Michael Faraday and Thomas Edison, and, of course, Norman Borlaug. There were social and political leaders like Napoleon, Lenin, Benito Mussolini, Thomas Jefferson and Adolf Hitler. Their accomplishments were not always for the benefit of mankind but they changed the world around them. There are also seminal events in history that have been initiated by change makers, including the French, American and Russian Revolutions. In fact, in any twist in history, especially if called a revolution, there will be a vanguard person.

We are here because of chance, fantastic luck. There is an old joke that goes "When I die I want to leave the world the same way I came in... by accident." The accident of our existence and the odds of our being here are truly astronomical. Just how improbable is it that we are here to contemplate the Universe? The Universe is like the lottery but the odds are more like one chance in ten with hundreds of zeros after it, a truly ineffable number. Each zero place holder adds a ten-fold increase in size. Almost certainly we should not be here... almost. If the evolution the Universe and of life is included and all factors combined, the odds of your existence are vanishingly close to zero.

Each one of us exists against impossible odds no matter how intelligent, cultured, bestial or ignorant. One must understand what an unthinkably huge coincidence that each and every one of us is and that we are each important. We live a very precarious life with forces acting to end our lives every second of our existence. All of your ancestors, every single one of them, back to the first amino acid that led to cellular life had to survive to reproduce. If there was a break in a single link of this multi-billion generational chain, you, humans or even all life on Earth would not exist. If you are reading this... Congratulations! You have beaten the astronomical odds of millions and millions of lotteries.

The numbers are so astronomical against our being here at this place and time, it would seem, that it is ultimate evil not to work toward a goal of being more than we are. Every human being should have a far greater destiny than being drug addled, a criminal, a corrupt politician or one of the ever-growing legions of government supported spouseless mothers and baby daddies. Humans need to be educated not propagandized. We need to be taught to be responsible. We need to make those impossible odds work in our favor and our descendants favor. It is about time that you, me... us, make those numbers count. Each one of us needs to appreciate the fact that we are truly significant and need to make a difference. We are the chosen ones. We can know this because of the amazing fact that we exist.

One has to admire our fellow humans; they are the end product of an incredible evolution. It is an extraordinary fact that a creature that had evolved for survival by using its brain to adapt masterfully to its environment could divine the workings of the Universe. About one hundred thousand years ago, all of humanity, the species of Homo sapiens, was a few thousand individuals and close to extinction. Somehow, these magnificent people managed to survive and everyone on earth is descended from them. We are truly all family. We are unique and deserve our day in the sun; we must now survive in the vast emptiness of the Universe. The question remains, who will be the hero or heroes that will lead us out to the greater Universe?